When Heartache Happens

A personal meditation of 1 Samuel 1

Pam Enderby

Come to the Fire Publishing

Dedicated to,
Jesus,
My merciful Savior,
Faithful Friend, and
Relentless Lover of my soul

From the publisher

Special thank you to Pam Enderby for donating all proceeds from this book to Come to the Fire ministry

ISBN
Printed in the United States of America
Published by Come to the Fire Publishing

PO Box 480052
Kansas City, MO 64148
cometothefire.org

Library of Congress Cataloging in Publication Data: ISBN 978-0-9838316-4-8
Printed in the United States of America

Contents

Introduction

What heartache are you facing? Your teen daughter's pregnancy? Your spouse says, "I don't love you anymore?" An aging parent needs constant care? A child chooses a rebellious lifestyle? Fragile finances? Infertility? The doctor has diagnosed a serious illness? Broken or strained relationships?

Troubles come in various forms. Elizabeth Elliot, best-selling author and former missionary, describes trouble as, "Having something you don't want, or wanting something you don't have."

Our enemy works hard to rob, steal, and destroy to attack physically, emotionally, mentally, or spiritually. (John 10:10) We feel helpless and grow hopeless as though we're caught in a bottomless pit. Our faith weakens, and we ask "Where is God?"

Longing for relief, what do we turn to for comfort, strength, and encouragement?

Lord of Hosts is calling to you. He desires to meet you face to face. He has the ability to turn your darkness into light. God will do for you what you can never do for yourself. He goes to impossible lengths to help!

These fourteen lessons will help you draw spiritual truths from Hannah's troublesome experiences. You will observe how God works His good and greater purposes in her life and how He can do the same for you. (1 Samuel 1-2) You'll discover God to be more precious than all your troubles. With His help, you will acquire freedom and inner peace.

F. B. Meyer states, "The iron crown of suffering precedes the golden crown of glory. And iron is entering into your soul to make it strong and brave."

When heartache happens:

1.Cultivate honesty and openness with God

2. Receive comfort in your loneliness

3.Discover God's good purposes for waiting

4.Receive grace to be and to do the impossible

5.Defeat unforgiveness...your biggest enemy

6.Embrace truth to derail your shame and squelch doubts about your true identity

7.Learn what to do with what-ifs and unanswered questions

8.Persevere in prayer and praise

9.Discover how to delight in God and merge your will into God's will

How to Use This Study

This study works best for personal Bible study. It is a devotional Bible study that includes real-life examples, questions for reflection, and space for journaling.

If you don't finish one lesson per sitting, don't fret! Keep in mind your goal is to discover peace and freedom. Allow the Holy Spirit to set your pace.

Please read 1 Samuel 1 daily before you begin each lesson.

Use the NIV translation to look for answers to questions unless advised otherwise. Biblegateway.com offers more translations.

The blank pages following each lesson are for journaling. Pay attention to what the Holy Spirit is teaching you. Record your feelings and Holy Spirit revelations. What you glean will comfort you and help you find freedom.

Troubles Visit Everyone

Today's verse

"I have told you these things, so that in me you may have peace. In this world you will have trouble. But take heart! I have overcome the world" (John 16:33).

Read: 1 Samuel 1

Hannah's arms ached to cradle a baby. She prayed, she wept, and she agonized. Yet, "the LORD had closed her womb."

To make matters worse, Hannah lived in a male-dominated society. A Jewish husband longed for a son to continue his family name. Since Hannah was barren society labeled her "worthless." A husband had the right to divorce a barren wife.

Second, God's law stated no woman "would be childless" if they were obedient. (Deuteronomy 7:14). Society would say Hannah was being punished by God.

Finally, Hannah's husband Elkanah, had another wife, Peninnah, who bore several children. She loved to rub it in, provoking Hannah to tears. Scripture says her stinging remarks "went on year after year."

Hannah doesn't pretend all is well. She doesn't deny or suppress her emotions, nor does she attempt to apply man-made solutions to fix her troubles. She clings to God. He is her Rock, her Fortress and Deliverer.

The first step to find freedom and peace when you're hurting is to admit your pain. Acknowledging your brokenness and the emotions it creates requires vulnerability. Sharing your thoughts and emotions with God will bond you to Him in a rich and meaningful way.

Heartfelt pain visits everyone. What is your heartache? What does God seem to be withholding from you?

In this lesson you will learn of others' difficulties. I trust it will prepare your heart to find freedom and peace.

Trouble in Marriage

I married with high, unrealistic expectations. I believed my husband would satisfy my every desire. My self-centered thoughts became filled with ugly arguments; my "prince charming" had failed. Three months into my marriage, I threatened divorce. I felt helpless and confused.

At that time, a newly wed insurance salesman and his wife befriended us. Their strong marriage boggled our minds. We wondered, *How can they be happy and at peace with each other when they have less than we do?*

Recognizing our spiritual needs, Tom and Sue began praying for us and they pointed us to Jesus. On November 7, 1974, my husband and I received Jesus Christ as our Savior. (Ephesians 1:13-14)

God used marriage troubles to fuel our desperation for Him. We learned about forgiveness and how to forgive. We began to pray together. God's Word gave us life-giving building blocks for a healthy marriage. God was cleaning and refining our hearts. Now, John and I counsel hurting marriages. This year, we celebrated our 41st wedding anniversary! (More on forgiveness in lessons 5-7!)

In 1 Corinthians 7:28, the apostle Paul points out an interesting truth about the marriage relationship. What does he say?

Psalm 119:67 offers hope regarding afflictions/heartache. Afflictions in marriage could be God's way of helping to build something beautiful in you.

Are you facing trouble in your marriage? Or perhaps a loved one experiences marriage troubles. How is it influencing you emotionally and mentally? How does it impact your relationship with God?

Trouble in Parenting

My husband and I committed to raising our children with love, understanding and discipline. Faithfully attending church and even squeezing in daily family devotions, I considered myself a good parent-until my teenagers rebelled. For a season, one child defiantly declared, "I don't want anything to do with your God" and another chose the "party life."

I felt devastated and condemned myself. I must have done something wrong. Where did I fail? I cried, prayed for my children to change and cried some more. Months turned into years of disappointment. Feeling rejected by my children hurt deeply. Fearful what-ifs plagued my mind. They tried hard to steal my peace and freedom! (Lesson 11 addresses what-ifs and unanswered questions).

My bedroom closet became my place of refuge. There, I learned to cry out to God and our friendship grew closer than any human friendship. Occasionally, I confided in a girlfriend. But pride and shame about what others would

14

think limited me. (Lesson 8 will help you demolish lies and squelch shame!)

Parenting troubles are remarkable opportunities to receive God's love and affirmation. God's magnificent grace is available to arm you with strength. (Lesson 4 will take you to the throne room of Grace. He empowers you to be and to do all that He calls you to be and all that He calls you to do—even with an aching heart). I learned God's good and greater purposes in waiting. (Lesson 12 offers insights about waiting. It is not in vain!)

Today, I continue to pray for my five adult children and praise God for all He has done in their lives. I pray they continue to be transformed into His image.

God has always been, and still is, the perfect Father! Often, we reject His ways which result in broken relationships. In Luke 12:49-53 Jesus describes such family relationships. How do you identify with them?

When I was experiencing parenting struggles, I learned that I don't need my kids to love me to believe God loves me. What thoughts and emotions do you battle?

Trouble in Other Relationships

A woman I was discipling grew angry with me when I tried to set healthy boundaries. "Please call me once a week rather than every day. I can talk for thirty minutes."

This woman hoped I'd change my mind. But I didn't. She labeled me "unforgiving" and "unloving" and spread hurtful rumors. Some church folks believed her. Their accusations played over and over in my mind, stealing my sleep and peace. That's when I leaned harder on God.

In the furnace of strained relationships, I experienced unexpected blessings. God's Word touched the depths of my heart and I grew to know Jesus' love better. I also learned how to forgive my enemies and walk in unconditional love. I recognized lies I had been believing about my identity. Renewing my mind with the truth about my identity in Christ set me free from deception's traps. (Embrace Your New Identity, lesson 9.)

Are you experiencing a troubling relationship with a family member or a church member? How is it influencing how you view yourself?

Physical Trouble

Dorothy suffers from various physical maladies, yet, she rejoices! She penned this spiritual song:
"You are too wonderful for me, Jesus,
Too wonderful for me, Lord.
You have placed Your hand on me,
Oh, Lord, how can this be?
Oh, Lord, you are too wonderful for me..."

In Revelation 2:9 what unusual phrase does the apostle John use to describe the believer who is suffering (NIV)?

How do you think you could be "rich" and afflicted at the same time?

Beth Coppedge, a keynote speaker for Come to the Fire, battled breast cancer. After Beth's sixth chemo treatment, several council members crowded into Beth's living room. Lying on her couch, Beth was suffering chemo's side effects, but she expressed a growing, passionate love for Jesus. She shared a vibrant message from God's Word. Her enthusiasm for personal and corporate revival had intensified. Beth was experiencing new intimacy with Jesus. Her eyes sparkled as she fondly remarked, "Jesus spoils me."

Praising God and delighting in Him while experiencing physical pain happens when you trust your heavenly Father is all wise and good.

What does Jesus promise in John 16:33? (More insight to come on this verse in Lesson 3.)

Let's press on! Look beyond what you see and feel. Jesus warned us not to be afraid to suffer. In partaking of "the fellowship of suffering with Christ" we can enter into the "power of His resurrection." (Phil. 3:10-11) Allow your faith to grow in God's great redemptive plan.

Dear Heavenly Father, life is difficult. Thank you for introducing me to others who have experienced sorrow and suffering. I am not alone. I am beginning to see how heartache can drive me to You and transformation begins. Please give me courage to face my heartaches. I desire fresh revelations from Your Word. Please pour out Your grace upon me. Give me wisdom and faith to apply what you teach me. I need You to walk with me each step of this journey. In Jesus name, Amen.

Truths to take away

1. No one is exempt from trouble. I am not alone in life's struggles and heartaches.

2. The first step to gain freedom and peace when I'm hurting is to honestly and openly confess my trouble to God.

3. Emotional, physical and spiritual distress can make my soul pliable and bendable. God is always close when my heart is aching. (Matthew 11:28-30)

Journal

Have You Received the Greatest Gift?

Today's verse

"God made Him who had no sin to be sin for us, so that in Him, we might become the righteousness of God" (2 Corinthians 5:21).

Read: 1 Samuel 1

Three times a year every Israelite male was required to worship and offer a sacrifice to the Lord. Hannah's misery was most intense when she went up to the tabernacle with Elkanah to worship. She wept constantly and began to refuse food. Regardless, she committed herself to faithful worship.

Clarke's Bible Commentary notes that Elkanah's sacrifices were probably peace-offerings when blood was poured out at the foot of the altar. The blood of the Old Testament sacrifices pointed forward to the blood of the Lamb of God. These sacrifices were types of the substance and reality to come. "The Jews of the Old Testament, then, were actually trusting in the Messiah and His work even though many of the details remained hidden from them."

Today, we believe in Christ as mediator and Savior of the new covenant. However, when heartache comes, you may doubt your salvation. This lesson will reinforce salvation truths to lead you toward greater freedom and peace.

The greatest gift

The path to healing begins with salvation. Humility is needed to admit your desperate need of God. To help you recognize your need, answer this question: "What must I do to be righteous (holy, perfect) as God is righteous?"

Remember that Jesus accomplished what you never could! "If man had his way, the plan of redemption would be an endless and bloody conflict. In reality, salvation was bought not by Jesus' fist, but by His nail-pierced hands; not by muscle but by love; not by vengeance but by forgiveness; not by force but by sacrifice. Jesus Christ our Lord surrendered in order that He might win; He destroyed His enemies by dying for them and conquered death by allowing death to conquer Him." (A. W. Tozer)

The following verses explain how Jesus has taken responsibility for satisfying God's displeasure of your sin. "We all, like sheep, have gone astray, each of us has turned to our own way; and the LORD has laid on _____ the _____ of us all," (Isaiah 53:6).

"Without the shedding of _____ there is no forgiveness" (Hebrews 9:22) or "remission" as stated in the NKJV.

Remission literally means "to send away." The word signifies release from bondage or imprisonment. It means canceling out all judgment, punishment and debt.

Meditate on Isaiah 53:4-5. "He [Jesus] took up our infirmities and carried our sorrows, yet we considered him stricken by God, smitten by him, and afflicted. But he [Jesus] was pierced for our transgressions, he [Jesus] was crushed for our iniquities; the punishment that brought us _____ was on him [Jesus], and by his [Jesus'] wounds we are _____." Explain why you don't have to resolve yourself of sin.

The great exchange

The apostle Paul clearly describes this act of love in 2 Corinthians 5:21a (MSG). "For God made Christ, who never sinned, to be an offering for our sin..." Explain why God did this according to 2 Corinthians 5:21b.

This great exchange declares you "righteous" in God's eyes. The word righteous means "to be approved, virtuous, faultless, accepted, and proclaimed not guilty." How is it possible to be made righteous according to Romans 4:4-5?

To be "righteous" is another way of saying, "You are forgiven. You are accepted by God." What does God's forgiveness promise according to Isaiah 43:25-26?

A young man who experienced a painful divorce was shunned by church people he had known as friends. They quit talking to him, and no one would sit by him in church. This same man felt more accepted by people in the world. Fortunately, he didn't forsake his faith. He received daily strength and encouragement by holding on to God's truth.

Why can you be certain God sees you "righteous" even when you're experiencing painful circumstances?

How the great exchange works

Think about this: when did Jesus die for your sins? Romans 5:8

Jesus didn't wait for you to become good enough before dying for you! To be approved or forgiven by God doesn't require pleading. What does it require? Ephesians 2:8-9

"No matter how hard you try to pay for your sins on your own-no matter how long you try to personally atone for them-it will never be enough. No amount of begging, suffering, or self-hate can do the job. There is only One who can take away the sin." Sheila Walsh

This gift of pardon, independent of your performance is a present wrapped in God's love and tied with the red ribbon of Christ's sacrifice. Jesus' blood makes you worthy and "_____ [you] us from all sin" (1 John 1:7).

You will be among the countless number of people standing in front of the throne and in front of the Lamb, dressed in a white robe and holding a palm branch in your hand, crying out in a loud voice: "Salvation belongs to our God, who sits on the throne, and to the Lamb" (Revelation 7:9-14).

Soak in the following truths. What has Jesus' blood accomplished for you?

__ *it justifies me and saves me from God's wrath* (Rom. 5:9). Jesus' violent death on the cross, shedding His blood, not keeping the law, put me in right standing before a Holy God.

___ *it brings me near to God* (Eph. 2:13). God raised me up to be seated with Christ "in the heavenly realms" (vs.6).
___ *it brings me peace and reconciliation to God* (Col. 1:20). I am declared, "not guilty!"
___ *it is the means by which I enter the most holy place with boldness* (Heb. 10:19). No shame or condemnation is greater than Jesus' blood.
___ *it sanctifies me* (Heb. 13:12). Jesus' blood has set me a part for His purposes by cleansing my conscience from acts that lead to death.
___ *it is the means by which I overcome the accuser of the brethren* (Rev. 12:11).

Does heartache cause you to doubt any of these salvation truths? It is time to put your full trust back in Jesus. What thoughts/feelings do you need to let go of that steal your freedom and peace?

Dear Lord Jesus, In the midst of all Your grand titles, You are also my Savior! Thank You for loving me while I was still a sinner. I exalt Your name, Lord. Thank you for sacrificing Yourself to provide complete forgiveness for my sins. Where would I be if You had not shed Your blood for me and freed me from the penalty and guilt of my sins? Thank you for the great exchange. Thank you that I am worthy and accepted in Your eyes even when I feel unworthy and unacceptable. Lord, You are the One who loves me with an everlasting love. You lead me and guide me with Your eye upon me. Impart to me, Lord, a fresh flow of joy. I celebrate who You are and what You have done for me. I now stand before You covered in Your love. I delight in your salvation. In Jesus' name, Amen.

Truths to take away

1. Jesus' shed blood on the cross is the greatest sacrifice. It's God's gift to me so that His wrath would be satisfied.

2. Trusting in Jesus' shed blood makes me right with God; it provides freedom from guilt, shame, and condemnation.

3. Believing the great exchange requires faith! "God made Him who had no sin to be sin for us, so that in Him, we might become the righteousness of God" (2 Corinthians 5:21).

Journal

Lesson 3

You Are Not Alone

Today's verse
 "My eyes are straining to see your promises come true.
When will you comfort me?" (Psalm 119:82 NLT)

Read: 1 Samuel 1

Hannah continues to pray and shed tears. Sorrow and grief fill her soul. Undoubtedly, Hannah is feeling rejected and lonely. Certainly it seems her world is falling apart.

Hannah understood that no one but the Lord could meet her needs or relieve her distress, so she clung to Him with all her strength. In this way she kept hope alive in an intolerable situation. She didn't pray for escape. She didn't plead for release from her marriage or for vengeance on spiteful Peninnah. She simply went on telling God her heart's desire, believing He had the ability to make the difference.

Can you be honest with God about how you really feel? Masking our emotions by saying "everything is O.K." is like putting a patch on an infected sore without first giving it proper medical attention.

Our Savior is intimately acquainted with your emotions. Our God goes beyond understanding. He

27

"knows" you! (Psalm 139) The Hebrew word for "know" is "yada." It conveys a deep emotional and experiential bonding between two people, such as when Adam knew Eve and they conceived a son. God knows you beyond intellectual knowing!

Today and always, the Lord rises to show you compassion (Isaiah 30:18). He is abundantly available! He never takes a break from His faithfulness. Will you open your heart to receive His comfort and compassion?

God's two favorite names

The word "trouble" (*thlipsis* in Greek) is used 45 times in the New Testament! It explodes with meaning: distress, hard circumstances, trials and suffering. Like carrying a load of bricks on your back, its weight is crushing. Hannah must have felt this kind of pressure.

Consider the Apostle Paul's troubles: beatings, imprisonments and riots, sleepless nights and hunger. (2 Corinthians 6:5) Paul didn't lose heart because God was renewing him from within. Evidence of this is how Paul addresses God.

What tender names does Paul use to address God and how do they reveal God was helping Paul? (2 Corinthians 1:3)

First, Paul praises the "God of all comfort." Comfort in the Greek language is translated paraclete. The Holy Spirit, also called the paraclete (John 14:16), is the "One called beside" you.

This truth bursts with meaning as I reflect upon my young child getting lost at the fair. For months afterward, 5-year-old Bonnie clung to my side. At the grocery store, the post office, and every public place, she hung on my sleeve, my pant leg, my coat. Bonnie was clinging just as the Holy Spirit clings to us!

Jesus makes a loving promise to you. "I will ask the Father, and He will give you another Counselor to _____" (John 14:16). Think of the Holy Spirit remaining your ever-present Comforter.

Young children instinctively turn to their parents in times of need. As a child of God, you have the privilege to cling to your heavenly Father. "Oh, love me—and right now!—hold me tight! Just the way you promised. Now comfort me so I can live, really live..." (Psalm 119:76 MSG).

The book of Jeremiah is filled with emotional descriptions of pain, awful predictions of disaster and sobering illustrations of suffering. Yet, God's undying love breaks through even the blackest hour. Meditate on Jeremiah 31:3: "The LORD has appeared of old to me, saying: 'Yes, I have loved you with an everlasting love; therefore with lovingkindness I have drawn you'" (NKJV). How does this truth about God's passionate love for His people comfort you?

Paul praises the "Father of compassion." The New Testament meaning for compassion is "to have mercy; to help one afflicted or seeking help." The Lord desires to show you mercy, to alleviate your distress while you are in the midst of trouble. When does the Lord show compassion? At selective times? Please carefully read Lamentations 3:19-24 and Psalm 9:9-10.

Does God place limitations on His compassion for you?

Why is it crucial, especially in the midst of heartache, to focus on your "Father of Compassion and God of all Comfort" remaining with you?

Pause to thank the Lord for continually offering unlimited compassion and comfort.

You are not alone

In John 16:33, Jesus shares these significant words before leaving His disciples, "…in me you may have peace. In this world you will have trouble [*thlipsis*]. But take heart! I have overcome the world."

The phrase, "you may have," in the original language is translated "to hold fast, to be closely joined to a person, to possess." When you feel troubles, pressures, alone and distant from God, you may have peace. Why? Because Jesus is closely joined to you. "…your right hand will hold me fast" (Psalm 139:10).

Write your name here. _____ is in Jesus; therefore Jesus is joined to me; Jesus is holding me fast and He will never leave me. Therefore, I may have _____.

In Psalm 91:1, God Almighty's name means "all-sufficient One." He is capable of providing all sufficient comfort and compassion. Isaiah 49:15 offers beautiful imagery to express your heavenly Father's tender closeness. Describe it.

Imagine a fretful infant needing nourishment. A mother pulls him to her breast and the disturbed child suddenly becomes quiet and satisfied. Your heavenly Father longs to hold you close as you would nestle your child close. (Psalm 131:2)

In Psalm 139:17-18 the ocean's sand granules are compared to God's precious thoughts of you! How many does He say there are?

God comforts in various ways: through Scripture, His whispers, music, other people. You will recognize His presence as it calms you, guides you, and gives you relief.

Be still and listen.What precious words is the God of all comfort and Father of compassion whispering to you?

The effect of Bonnie getting lost caused her to wake from sleep with panic-fear. She shrieked my name into the darkness and I came running to her bedside. Bonnie's cries made a powerful appeal for my comfort and prayers. Depend on it that God your heavenly Father hears your cries. You will never call out in vain.

God's closeness and willingness is revealed to you in Isaiah 41:10. What is He saying to you?

I am

I am

I will

I will

Lorraine is living in the reality of these truths. Her 16-year-old daughter was kidnapped and brutally murdered. Lorraine says, "When at our lowest point, if we reach up and take God's hand, everything changes. Only He could take this tragedy and turn it to good."

Jesus understands your grief and sorrow. He is your Savior "a man of sorrow, and acquainted with grief" (Isaiah 53:3). How does Jesus assure you He understands your sorrow? Read Hebrews 4:15.

Freedom and rest comes as you abandon your pride and roll your painful emotions onto God. Crying out to God stops that ugly poison from spreading or becoming deeply rooted. Crying tears of guilt over regrettable mistakes rids guilt from growing into depression, anxiety, or physical distress. Crying tears over sorrowful losses prepares your soul for the Lord's tender touch.

David laments, "I am exhausted as I groan; all night long I drench my bed in tears; my tears saturate the cushion beneath me" (Psalm 6:6 NET). How does the Lord respond? (See verses 8b-9.)

Jeremiah laments, "Streams of tears flow from my eyes because my people are destroyed. Tears flow from my eyes and will not stop; there will be no break until the LORD looks down from heaven and sees what has happened" (Lamentations 3:48-49 NET). How does the Father of compassion respond? He rushes to Jeremiah's side. His heart is moved and offers him relief. Jeremiah continues, "You have heard my plea; 'Do not close your ears to my cry for relief!' You came near on the day I called to you; you said, 'Do not fear!'" (Verses 56-57)

The Father of compassion sees your sorrow, grief and suffering. He rushes to your side when you call to Him. Write your worries and troubles on the empty pages provided. Your heavenly Father is waiting to hear from you.

Dear Lord, You know I am hurting. Please wrap me in Your strong, loving arms. May I feel Your love, comfort, and compassion. Thank you for never being too tired to listen; for never interrupting, for never giving unwarranted advice, for never growing weary or frustrated with me when I don't make sense or when I come to you repeatedly with my pain. Thank you for peace awaiting me. Right now, I pour out my heart to You. Amen.

Truths to take away

1. The Holy Spirit's presence remains with me to strengthen, encourage and comfort.

2. My heavenly Father rises with compassion when He hears my cry for help.

3. Jesus understands my grief and sorrow and responds to my tears.

Journal

Journal

Grace—God's Power to Be and to Do

Today's verse

"My grace is sufficient for you, for my power is made perfect in weakness" (2 Corinthians 12:9).

Read: 1 Samuel 1

Hannah's name means "grace" and rightly so. Fainthearted Hannah could not change her circumstances, but she could admit her needs and her insufficiencies and cling to the Lord. In doing so, God's work of grace strengthened her. It delivered her from harboring animosities and from retaliating.

Jesus offers you grace. Day after day, no matter how difficult your relationships, how painful your circumstances, how insufficient your finances, how weak your will power, or how lacking your confidence, even the smallest drop of God's grace is more than enough. It transforms "Why Me, Lord?" to " You *are* with me, Lord!"

Grace does not diminish troubles. It causes you to realize God will go to impossible lengths to help you. Grace makes it possible to find freedom and peace.

Grace is a gift

Hannah continually asked the Lord of Hosts for a son. He answered "no." God's desire was for Hannah to receive His gift of grace. He was calling Hannah to a deeper dependence upon Him. "My grace is sufficient for you, for _____ is made perfect in _____" (2 Corinthians 12:9).

Read *The Amplified Version*. "My grace—My favor and loving-kindness and mercy—are enough for you, [that is, sufficient against any danger and to enable you to bear the trouble manfully]; for My strength and power are made perfect-fulfilled and completed and show themselves most effective-in [your] weakness."

What key words stand out in this verse?

With this definition in mind consider Hannah's marriage. She lived with Peninnah, the "other woman" in a competitive, unsatisfying marriage. How might Hannah have reacted to Peninnah's ongoing jibes if grace had not empowered her?

Then her husband tried to soothe Hannah by offering her a double portion of meat. When his attempt failed, he questions her, "Don't I mean more to you than 10 sons?" (vs. 5, 8). If grace had not held Hannah's tongue, how might she have responded?

Grace may not change your circumstances, but it will offer divine power to change you within. In my early years of marriage, I kept a mental record of my husband's wrongs for petty things like: he doesn't help with the housework, he leaves his clothes on the floor, he spends too much time pastoring others, he doesn't thank me for washing and ironing his clothes. I'd pout, cry, and get angry. I'd act like a martyr. I'd wish I'd married someone else. I'd give him the silent treatment. I'd feel I was too good for him.

I prayed that God would change him, but He didn't. So I tried to change him and that instigated more tension. One day after complaining to God about how bad off I was, His gentle yet firm words stopped me. "I can help you if you are willing to change."

I wanted our marriage to work; I had made a vow to John to love and honor him in sickness and health, for better or for worse. I made that vow in the presence of God and didn't want to leave him for minor annoyances.

I began to ask God to forgive me. I asked God for His strength, guidance, and wisdom concerning the changes I needed to make. As I continued to pray, I realized how my immaturity had almost spoiled our marriage. My husband had never done anything immoral or horrible.

God's work of grace in my life helped me let go of my husband's irritations. I realized what a good man he is. I now felt peace, relief, and gratitude.

One Bible teacher states, "Grace is a word the Bible uses to describe God's commitment to change us-to reshape us into the image of Christ." You cannot change yourself; however, grace can.

Have you thought, *If God would only change that person or thing, I'd be happy?* God is able to give you something better than improving your situation or changing that person. Repeat this truth: I chose to believe God's grace is sufficient for _____ [insert your name here.]

The promise of grace to do "immeasurably more" is stated in Ephesians 3:20. Write it here and post it where you'll see it throughout the day.

A miracle of grace

Who are you depending upon?

Are you weary?

Do you need rest from your troubles?

The Lord sees your weariness. He calls you to rest a while!

Rest seemed out of the question for Philip. When thousands of men, women and children came to hear Jesus teach and Jesus saw their hunger, He asked Philip, "Where shall we buy bread for these people to eat?" What feelings and thoughts do you think Philip had? (John 6:5)

If you were in Philip's sandals and Jesus asked you that question, how would you have responded?

Heartache may indicate a greater measure of God's grace is awaiting you. Little did the disciples know Jesus was positioning them for a miracle of grace! Perhaps the Lord is positioning you for a miracle of grace.

Jesus took the two fish and five loaves and "gave thanks." (vs.11) What did He ask the Father to do with the little He had? How did God manifest His grace? (vs.12-13)

Who or what is your source of help? Are you looking to yourself, someone else, or something other than God? Why?

Do you feel an urgency to remain emotionally strong for others? Why?

Perhaps God is gently nudging you to get out of the way so that He can show Himself strong. What might you have to let go of? Stop thinking? Stop doing?

What keeps you from depending upon Jesus?

"The soul life will always seek to oppose and quench the Holy Spirit by leaning upon its own strength without wholly relying upon God's grace. The soulish realm has enormous energies of self-will, including self-pity, self-love, and the fear of suffering, with the prime motivation being self-preservation. It will always fight against taking the cross and dying to self-centeredness. Only the Holy Spirit, through prayer, can empower us to die to self-will." (Watchman Nee, *The Spiritual Man*)

Self-preservation often looks like trying to be in control. Feeling the insecurity of being out of control leads to the unreasonable desire for control.

When the lady I was discipling was growing emotionally dependent upon me, fire alarms went off in my head. Unfortunately, I couldn't help her see the truth about her unhealthy dependence. She retaliated. She gossiped her grievances to others in the church, including a few church leaders, and several took her side.

The situation grew messier as Satan spread his poison. Private meetings were held behind my back to discuss my "unforgiving, unloving behavior." I could see the ship was sinking—our church, and all its precious treasures: close friendships, financial comfort, and a good reputation among my peers.

My husband and I did all we could in our own strength to preserve what we thought was God's will. We phoned and emailed friends, trying to explain our side... the truth. We begged God to open blind eyes to truth. We tried to fix the mounting problems.

I panicked; our desire and efforts to make everything right failed. I questioned God, why don't you allow the truth to be known? Why do you let your church look bad to an unsaved world? Why do you let this happen to us? God wastes nothing. He allowed this suffering, and He since has used it for His glory. He "makes everything work out according to his plan" (Ephesians 1:11).

The months that followed my pastor husband's resignation served to draw me closer to Jesus. He became more to me than Someone I served. He became my intimate Friend. He embraced my heart of grief. It felt like He was holding my hand each step of the healing way. I experienced His presence in worship like never before. He never left me or forsook me. (Hebrews 13:5) I learned obedience from what I suffered (Hebrews 5:8). I learned a hard lesson: never try to please man above myself or God.

God's grace will help you surrender to the place and position He has given you. He desires rest for you and your freedom to give up control. "I have been crucified with Christ," Paul writes, "and I no longer live, but Christ lives in me. The life I live in the body, I live by faith in the

Son of God, who loved me and gave himself for me" (Galatians 2:20).

Are you willing to turn over your unfair situation to God and any injustice that was done to you? Describe any behavior that expresses your desire for control or the desire to please yourself more than God.

Where and how to receive grace

Be aware! Satan would have you pretend, put on a happy face, and strive to fix your troubles. He'll instigate shame and unworthiness to keep you away from the One Who offers grace in your time of need. One believer shared, "I had disappointed God so I didn't feel worthy; I hid from Him. So I struggle to enter the throne of grace." Feeling good about yourself is not God's prerequisite to enter His presence. According to the truths of Romans 5:7-10, why can you freely enter God's throne room of grace?

In what fashion are you encouraged to draw near to God in your time of need? Hebrews 4:14-16.

After the painful church situation, I had learned to lean hard on the power of God's grace. One morning I wrote:

"Dear Lord, I need Your grace to emotionally release my (grown) children to make mistakes without worrying about them or interfering. I need grace to unconditionally love a difficult woman in my church because I'd rather ignore her. I need Your grace to trust You for financial provision instead of looking to people as my source of security. I need grace to keep praying in faith for my father when it seems like his heart will never change. I need Your grace to fix my eyes on You instead of myself."

Being honest with God about my needs activated the fullness of His grace to work. His Spirit guided me to His promises: 2 Corinthians 9:8 and Philippians 4:13, 19.

I encourage you to read them out loud and paraphrase the one that is most meaningful to you.

Twenty-year-old Annie McVay gave permission to share her testimony that illustrates God's beautiful grace at work.

God has brought me through 18 surgeries, years of chronic back pain, 2 seasons of seizures, periods of deafness and blindness, diagnosed chronic fatigue, a year of intense migraines, and nearly a decade of struggling with severe, life threatening asthma.

At times, my day consisted of waking up, eating breakfast, taking medicine, lying down, getting dressed, going to a doctor's appointment, coming home, taking medicine, eating lunch, doing home school, lying down, talking with my siblings, eating dinner, taking medicine, lying down, reading the Bible with my mom, and then going to bed. This is an exhausting day for the chronically ill person.

I learned to live with chronic pain and fatigue from a young age. I had few friends. I had few aspirations. I didn't know why God wasn't healing me. I didn't understand why I should live this way while everyone else had a "real" childhood and adolescence. They went to birthday parties; they played outside. They didn't wake up and rate their present pain. My mother did an incredible job of making life enjoyable for me in other ways, but it wasn't the same.

I received prayer for healing continuously. Every Sunday, for years, my pastor laid hands on me and prayed for the asthma and scoliosis and seizures to go away. Every Sunday, I

swallowed my disappointment. I knew God could heal me if He
wanted to. Psalm 103:2-4 says, "Bless the Lord, O my soul, and
forget not all his benefits, who forgives all your iniquity, who
heals all your diseases, who redeems your life from the pit, who
crowns you with steadfast love and mercy." I believe every word
of that psalm. I know that He is able; I know that I am willing.
He does forgive my iniquity. He does redeem my life from the pit.
He does crown me with steadfast love and mercy. So, why is it I
don't get healing from all my diseases? If the others are true, why
has this one not happened?

I believe it is God's will to heal. I have even experienced it
(majestically) a couple times. But that's not what I'm here to talk
about today, because I believe my testimony of illness is far
greater than my testimony of health. Yes. I believe that God's will
for me to be weak has and will continue to touch many lives.

My life changed dramatically once I read 2 Corinthians 12
and let these Scriptures seep into my soul like a tea bag. (I steep
my tea indefinitely.) "But He said to me, 'My grace is sufficient
for you, for my power is made perfect in weakness.' Therefore, I
will boast all the more gladly of weaknesses, so that the power of
Christ may rest upon me. For the sake of Christ, then, I am
content with weaknesses, insults, hardships, persecutions, and
calamities. For when I am weak, then I am strong."

This passage was revolutionary for me! I was struggling to
breathe and not tire out while hiking with my family on Turkey
Mountain (west Tulsa wilderness). We'd been going about ten
minutes and I was about ready to turn around. David was
reciting Scripture and got excited for a moment. "Ooooh! Annie!
I read the perfect Scripture for you. I think it's going to be your
life verse. It's a little paradoxical, but that's normal with our
God." David always has Scripture to encourage me, so I didn't
think anything of it at the time. But as we hiked and he mulled
over its meaning, I began to feel empowered. "When I am weak,
then I am strong." That shouldn't work. I shouldn't get to be
stronger when I'm weaker. Aren't they opposites?

The next few weeks God put me on spiritual dialysis as I thought and prayed this verse in to my life. My embarrassment began to fade. I no longer shied away from conversations about my sickness. In fact, I did start to "boast" all the more "gladly" in my weaknesses. I would wake up weary and smile, thinking to myself, "God wants me to have HIS strength today!" I'd proudly ask for help to the bathroom, knowing that God wanted to give my family the opportunity to serve.

My outlook on chronic illness shifted greatly. This was not a life that had been "cursed" by the devil. This was a life God wanted credit for! He wants to put His Power in me each and every day so that people will know how strong He is. If He can keep a fragile little thing like me alive and smiling, He can certainly work out your marital problems! He can most definitely help you pass that class. If my bronchioles can totally constrict and send my body into code blue respiratory distress, but my God keeps me conscious just long enough to receive treatment, what can't He do?

Isn't it cool that I've learned to fight the natural instincts of death while I wait for God to pull me through to the next breath? I think it's exhilarating to live this life. Who has total recollection of seizure events? Who can tell you every thing the Holy Spirit whispered to her while her body convulsed for minutes? Who boasts in their weaknesses? I do! All the more gladly! Because I know that by doing so, the Power of Christ rests upon me.

All the glory and power be to Him

Annie might say that spending "one day" in the presence of God is better than spending thousands of days in the absence of trouble: Drawing upon God's grace, our relationship with Him flourishes. (Psalm 84:10-11)

Let's end today's lesson with honest confession and prayer.

Dear Heavenly Father, Thank you for unlimited grace. Help me to be still and soak in the truth that Your grace is stronger than my weaknesses. I surrender my determination and control. By faith, I release my grip and expectation on anyone or anything to help me, except the Lord Jesus. I believe He is able to make all grace abound to me in all things and at all times, having all that I need in every good work. In Jesus' name, Amen."

I need God's gift of grace for... (Remember to include anyone or any situation you've been trying to control. You may use the empty pages following this lesson.)

Truths to take away

1. Jesus knows what I am going through and offers generous amounts of grace. (Hebrews 4:15, 16)

2. Receiving God's grace establishes rest within and freedom from fears.

3. Grace doesn't promise the absence of struggle, but the presence of God. Grace transforms me from within to bring me through my trouble.

Journal

Your Biggest Enemy— Unforgiveness

Today's verse

"Lord, how many times shall I forgive my brother when he sins against me? … Jesus answered, 'I tell you, not seven times, but seventy-seven times'" (Matthew 18:21-22).

Read: 1 Samuel 1

Human instinct is to take revenge, be angry, remain bitter, or withdraw. Hannah knew resentful words and behavior would instigate more broken relationships so she made it her priority to not allow others' actions and attitudes determine hers.

Has someone hurt you? It may be something done against you; it may be what someone didn't do or say. Do you entertain negative thoughts, attitudes, and feelings toward others?

Unforgiveness is one of our biggest enemies. Unforgiveness blocks God's love, compassion and mercy. It puts us in bondage and keeps us from experiencing freedom and peace.

Today, consider how you respond when others hurt you. Consider forgiveness to be a journey away from hatred.

During Nazi occupations in Holland, Corrie Ten Boom and her family were sent to a concentration camp for hiding Jews. Millions of people were tortured, raped, and burned to death. Guards enjoyed seeing the horror and humiliation. Corrie came to hate the guard who mocked and sneered at their naked bodies when the women were taken to the showers. His terrible face was branded in her memory. Her sister, Betsy, succumbed to the abuse and died, but Corrie survived and promised never to return to Germany.

Many years later, she did return for a speaking engagement where she taught on forgiveness. To her shock, the same guard was sitting in the church. He could never have recognized Corrie as one of the sick, shaved, and nearly starved prisoners in his camp. His radiant face even suggested that he had since become a believer. After the talk, the guard approached her. With a smiling face he extended his hand and said, 'Ah, dear sister Corrie, isn't it wonderful how God forgives?'

At that moment, all the hatred surged up in Corrie-the grief of a thousand wrongs for the evil he had done to her and her beloved family. Suddenly the Lord said, 'Corrie, put out your hand.' This was the hardest step of obedience Corrie had ever faced, but she put out her hand. After that act of submission, she testified: 'I felt something almost like warm oil being poured over me. And with it came the unmistakable message: Well done, Corrie. That's how my children behave. Since that moment, the hate was totally gone.

Carefully read Ephesians 4:32. Jesus teaches your responsibility is to forgive. Why is it essential?

"Forgiveness is a key that unlocks the door of resentment and the handcuffs of hatred. It is the power that breaks the chains of bitterness and the shackles of selfishness," said Corrie Ten Boom. Forgiveness is your pathway to freedom and peace. If you practice unforgiveness into whose hands do you put your emotional health?

Consider the dangers of unforgiveness

Forgiveness doesn't excuse others' behavior or condone their wrong or hurtful action. Forgiveness prevents their behavior from destroying your heart.

When I turned 19, my parents filed for divorce. Leaving the courtroom my father stormed after me. Pointing his finger, he glared and snarled, "From now on I'll never be your father." The break in our relationship was not my fault, but it still caused deep pain and loneliness.

I carried the anguish of rejection and abandonment for a long time. Resentment, anger and self-pity, all flesh responses, waged war within my spirit. I didn't feel like forgiving my father. I held onto my hurt to in some way protect me from more pain. "The mind of sinful man is death, but the mind controlled by the Spirit is life and peace" (Romans 8:6).

Thankfully, one day, Hebrews 12:14-15 captured my heart. "See to it that _____ misses the _____ of God and that no _____ _____ grows up to cause trouble and defile many."

Withholding forgiveness is Satan's deceptive trap. Practicing unforgiveness multiplied my emotional and mental trouble. After confessing my need for help, the Holy Spirit faithfully stepped in. He led me to the truths below that strengthened my spirit and fortified my trust in Him. Consequently, I chose to forgive my father.

How does Psalm 35:1 explain God will be your Judge?

How will you demonstrate trust in God as your Judge rather than making personal judgments against those who hurt you?

How does Psalm 18:1-2 and Psalm 91:1-3 explain God as your defender and refuge?

How will you demonstrate trust in God as your Defender and Refuge rather than defend yourself inappropriately?

Meditating on these truths, I reached out to my father in love, even with an aching heart. I phoned him and wrote him friendly letters. Again and again, he rejected me. His position has remained strong, "I'll never be your father."

A.W. Tozer states, "Instead of cringing under every criticism, smarting under each slight, tossing sleepless if another is preferred, let's give up the fight."

Bitterness is love's enemy. Bitterness is a root that produces rotten, sickly fruits. (Matthew 7:17) Consider the bad fruit mentioned in Colossians 3:5-9: sexual immorality, lying, anger, slander, lust, evil desires, rage, greed, idolatry, filthy language. If you are not practicing forgiveness, what negative behavior/feelings may be growing in you?

How do they affect you, your family, others?

The unmerciful servant

Please carefully read the parable of the unmerciful servant. Matthew 18:21-35.

What serious consequence awaited the first servant who couldn't pay his debt? Ten thousand talents equals millions of dollars today!

Fortunately, the master showed his servant mercy. How do you relate to the servant about your forgiven debts? (Perhaps recall the truths in Lesson 2 to remind you of how much God has forgiven you.)

That same servant then went out trying to collect a "debt" someone owed him. It amounted to a hundred denarii or ten thousand dollars today. What did the master do to the unforgiving servant?

Are you trying to collect "debts" that others owe you? What emotional and mental danger are you putting yourself in?

This parable precedes Jesus' instructions about when to forgive others. "Lord, how many times shall I forgive my brother when he sins against me? Up to seven times?" Peter asked. How did Jesus answer in Matthew 18:21-22?

In other words, never stop forgiving. Unforgiveness is burdensome, too heavy to bear. Medical research reports people with pent-up bitterness and inner hostility show a propensity for high blood pressure, impaired immune function, muscle spasms, hormonal changes, memory loss, and increased heart attacks. Our freedom and peace depend upon choosing forgiveness.

Heavenly Father, Thank you for showing me the freedom of forgiving. You understand how I allow my emotions to control me and then I withhold forgiveness. I don't want anyone but You to control my actions and emotions. Please reveal anything that keeps me from granting forgiveness. I want to love others and experience freedom and peace. In Jesus name. Amen.

Truths to take away

1. Forgiveness is the key to maintain and cultivate fellowship and close communion with God.

2. Forgiveness is a decision to obey God and walk in love, not allowing others to determine my actions or attitudes.

3. Jesus commands me to offer unlimited forgiveness. Otherwise, I'll fall prey to Satan's schemes. Jesus supplies grace to forgive unlimited times. "Lord, how many times shall I forgive my brother when he sins against me? Jesus answered, 'I tell you not seven times, but seventy-seven times'" (Matthew 18:21-22).

Hindrances to Walking in Forgiveness

Today's verse

"...let us throw off everything that hinders and the sin that so easily entangles, and let us run with perseverance the race marked out for us" (Hebrews 12:1).

Read: 1 Samuel 1

Today let's carefully consider three major hindrances to walking in forgiveness.

Pride

Hannah desired to please God rather than hold onto her pride. She was not argumentative or defensive. There was not a trace of self-centeredness, which is an indicator of pride.

Based upon James 4:6, please write how God responds to a prideful person.

The word "oppose" in Greek has a military meaning: "to rage in battle against." God powerfully comes against pride. "Though the Lord is great, he cares for the humble, but he keeps his distance from the proud (Psalm 138:6). Who wants to be resisted by God?

According to Isaiah 59:2, how does pride affect your prayers?

Anger

Anger is a natural and often automatic response to heartache. Hannah had a right to be angry; she was mistreated, annoyed, and irritated. But she didn't display anger.

What does God's Word tell you to do when you are angry?

Ephesians 4:26

James 1:19-20

A woman had a terrible time controlling her temper. This caused her to throw kitchen utensils in all directions. A pastor visited her and said, "You may not stop yourself from getting angry, but close your fists real tight and lift them up to God alone. Then open your hands and release the anger to Him. Let Him make things right." Within a matter of months, this woman was free from a lifelong habit of violent flare-ups.

Do you feel angry because you think you deserve something, and you are not getting it?

Do you feel your rights are being violated?

If you hold onto your right to be angry you prolong and complicate your journey to freedom and peace. One teacher said "Most believers have dealt with their wrongs, but what they really need to do is nail their rights to the Cross."

Self-righteousness

Self-righteousness blinds us to our faults and failures. We think we are right and others are wrong.

One day Jesus heard his disciples arguing about who was the greatest. (Luke 22:26-27) Does His answer apply to you as well? Why or why not?

For millenniums people have prided themselves on fasting, tithing and other spiritual rituals. Has this kind of spiritual self-righteousness crept into your life?

Self-righteousness creates a barrier between you and the Lord. Consider the following:

Do you gossip?

Do you hold back from others with a critical spirit?

Do you act with an indifferent attitude?

What did Jesus express in Luke 6:42?

It feels impossible to forgive

In some situations, the offense is so agonizing, we feel, "It's impossible to forgive." Hannah is a beautiful example of choosing to forgive, again and again, while being misunderstood and belittled.

Nancy also faced an "unforgivable" situation. Yet Jesus showed Nancy the way to forgiveness. Here is her story as she told it.

My husband was unfaithful to me. He had a secret affair which I suspected for about a year. During that time he lied to me about it as if nothing was going on.

Finally, proof was brought to my attention and I decided to confront him. Full of bitterness and anger, I wanted to shame him with nasty words!

But when that moment came, face to face with him, suddenly I saw the cross with Jesus' outstretched hands....bleeding. I became so powerless....nothing came out of my mouth as I had planned.

I heard a voice. "I am a forgiving God, gracious, compassionate, slow to anger and abounding in love" (Neh. 9:17).

I told my husband, "I am forgiven, so you are forgiven!"

He looked at me, puzzled.

God graciously helped me to be crucified with Him on the Cross. "I no longer live but Christ lives in me" (Galatians 2:20).

Then I asked my forgiven husband to take me where the woman and child lived. (They had a child together.)

When I saw the woman and their child, I could hug them.

I kissed the little girl as if she were my own. Christ reigned and controlled me!

Ever since that day, I am set free to forgive people easily, without struggle! Because Christ lives through me, I'm able to fellowship with my ex-husband and his wife as my brother and sister in Christ without any consciousness of the past.

Consider another saint who endured an agonizing experience and found it possible to forgive. Stephen was sentenced to being stoned. (Acts 7:54-60) If Stephen had based forgiveness on his feelings, how would his last moments before death have been different?

By allowing hurt feelings to dictate whether or not you will forgive, it will be impossible to let go of anger or resentments. How did Nancy and Stephen find the willingness to forgive?

You may feel cheated and struggle with emotions that won't let go of the offense or you want to take revenge. The battle is in full swing. (Galatians 5:17) If you walk in the flesh, you will lose. What are your most common excuses for not walking in forgiveness? Pride? Anger? Self-righteousness? Explain.

Jesus will help you release the offense so you can bless those who have hurt you. This is not humanly possible, but with Jesus' divine help "_____ _____ are possible" Matthew 19:26.

If you desire God's help, what must you do?

"Now to Him who is able to keep you from stumbling, and to make you stand in the presence of His glory blameless with great joy, to the only God our Savior, through Jesus Christ our Lord, be glory, majesty, dominion and authority, before all time and now and forever. Amen" (Jude 1:24-25).

What if I am in an abusive relationship?

Dr. Bill Maier, a Focus on the Family's counselor, suggests, "Find a supportive counselor who can help you develop a plan to confront the abuser and protect yourself. Our counseling department at Focus on the Family can refer you to a licensed Christian therapist in your community who has experience in dealing with domestic abuse."

Focus on the Family recommends the following books: *Wounded by Words: Healing the Invisible Scars of Emotional Abuse* by Susan Titus Osborn, Karen L. Kosman, Jeenie Gordon. The authors explore how emotional abusers isolate, disorient, and indoctrinate their victims and how their unkind words leave lasting scars. Sharing stories of people from the Bible and from contemporary life who have suffered verbal abuse, the authors offer tested, scriptural advice for breaking the cycle.

Angry Men and the Women Who Love Them: Breaking the Cycle of Physical and Emotional Abuse by Paul Hegstrom. This book is an invaluable aid for the man who batters, the woman who feels trapped, and the pastor, counselor, or friend who desperately wants to help them both.

Precious Lord, Thank you for revealing my pride. I desire to be humble like You. I tend to argue, and I am defensive. Please help me to listen and be open-hearted to correction. I need your help to embrace the power of humility. Often I'm angry on the inside, and I explode on the outside. Please help me with self-control. I want to radiate joy instead of anger and forgiveness instead of spite. Sometimes I judge others in an unkind way. I am sorry for gossiping. Please continue to prepare my heart to apply the grace of forgiveness. In Jesus name, Amen.

Truths to take away

1. Self-centeredness is a character trait of pride which God strongly resists.

2. Holding onto my right to be angry prolongs my journey to freedom and peace.

3. Offering forgiveness is possible when I ask Jesus for His help.

Journal

Applying the Grace of Forgiveness

Today's verse
"Forgive as the Lord forgave you" (Colossians 3:13).

Read: 1 Samuel 1

Hannah's relationship with God flourished because she generously applied forgiveness. It's our Great Physician's remedy for pride, anger, self-righteousness and other sins. Freedom and peace follow.

To apply the grace of forgiveness may take several sittings. Be patient as you wait upon the Holy Spirit to lead you.

The help of the Holy Spirit

During my teens' rebellion, their words and actions cut deep. I realized my need to forgive them, but I stubbornly held onto resentment. I replayed hurtful words and actions over and over in my mind. I thought, they don't deserve my forgiveness.

Then the Holy Spirit revealed this truth. While hanging on the cross, Jesus said, "Father forgive them..." In other words, Jesus was telling His heavenly Father, "I need You to do the forgiving through Me."

Thereafter, many times a day, I prayed, "Father, I want You to forgive my child through me. I desire to become a channel for Your forgiveness." That approach helped me to forgive.

Compassion replaced bitter resentment. My heart was no longer held captive to sin's bondage. Now, I could view my children caught in Satan's clutches rather than obstinate teenagers trying to make my life miserable. With God's heart, I was now free to lovingly pray for them.

Enforcing healthy boundaries in love rather than anger never pleased my kids. But this new spirit of love that controlled me nurtured freedom and peace in all of us.

Applying the grace of forgiveness

You can begin to apply the grace of forgiveness with prayer.

Heavenly Father, Pour out Your Holy Spirit upon me in a fresh way. Shine Your light into the corners of my heart. Reveal any unforgiveness I'm harboring. Allow Your mercy to fall upon me. Empower me against dark spiritual forces. I want nothing to keep me from experiencing your freedom and peace. Thank you that Your grace, always has been and always will be enough. In Jesus' name, Amen.

Steps to apply the grace of forgiveness

Following these steps may help you stay focused. Patiently allow the Holy Spirit to lead you. He enlightens the mind. Humility is His method.

1. Ask the Holy Spirit to access the hurt places of your heart. Only He can detect pride, selfishness, anger and other ways your flesh keeps you in bondage. "Search me,

God, and know my heart; test me and know my anxious thoughts. See if there is any offensive way in me, and lead me in the way everlasting" (Psalm 139:23-24).

2. Write down wrong attitudes, actions, and words which others have used to hurt you.

3. Ask the Holy Spirit to help you offer forgiveness to each one with no strings attached. Remember, the person who hurt you doesn't have to earn forgiveness.

Forgiveness is a gift! As Christ's child, no one's sin, not even your own, has the right to hold you captive. Use this prayer to guide you: Lord, I forgive _____.

Lord, I give You permission to take the judgment, the unforgiveness and the bitterness out of me. I am sorry it has taken root. I do not want this in my life any longer. I surrender it all to You. Please show me if I contributed to this sin done against me. I choose to no longer blame or hold onto what _____ did to me. I surrender my right to be paid back for my loss by _____. I declare my trust in You alone, Lord God, as Righteous Judge and Redeemer.

Father God, bless _____ in every way. From now on, I promise to speak and think only good about him/ her. In Jesus' name, Amen.

If the enemy reminds you of the hurt, say, "Jesus has forgiven that through me. His forgiveness is my forgiveness."

4. Allow time for the Holy Spirit to help you work through your feelings. Experience His healing. Release your hurts to God (1 Peter 2:21-23). A trusted friend or counselor may assist you to access more of God's healing power and truth.

5. Listen for God's response. Is He speaking Scripture to you? Is He instructing you to make amends? Pray for your offender? (Matthew 5:44). Perhaps pray, "Lord, show me how you view this person."

6. Now give thanks for God's mercy and grace. Intentionally fill the empty places in your heart with God's

Word and praise. "If I had cherished sin in my heart, the Lord would not have listened; but God has surely listened and heard my voice in prayer. Praise be to God, who has not rejected my prayer or withheld his love from me!" (Psalm 66:18-20)

You can know you have truly forgiven when you no longer expect anything from your offender-no validation, amends or recognition. One teacher sums it up like this, "Forgiveness is complete when you are at peace whenever you think of your offender."

Keep your newfound freedom and peace by applying the grace of forgiveness to new hurts and new offenses.

Truths to take away

1. By allowing the Holy Spirit to access the hurt places of my heart, He will detect pride, selfishness, anger and other ways I have catered to my flesh.

2. Applying the grace of forgiveness requires prayer, patience, and perhaps professional help.

3. Allowing the Father to forgive through me brings freedom and peace to my soul and blessings to others.

Journal

Overcome Shame

Today's verses

"In you, O Lord, I put my trust; Let me never be ashamed; Deliver me in Your righteousness. Bow down Your ear to me; deliver me speedily; be my rock of refuge; a fortress of defense to save me" (Psalm 31:2-3).

Read: 1 Samuel 1

Undoubtedly Hannah felt shame. She must have heard, "You're barren because God is punishing you for some sin." Perhaps Hannah heard it so often that, like an abused child, she felt that maybe she deserved it. When Hannah "wept and would not eat" (verse 7), when she was "in bitterness of soul" (verse 10), and when she stated, "I am a woman who is deeply troubled" (Verse 15), could have been the result of feeling shame. Shame easily weaves its way into a person's soul when emotional and physical neglect occurs.

Have *you* heard shame's voice? *If you had been a better person or done something differently, this wouldn't have happened.*

A common response to shame is to erect a façade and hide, as Adam and Eve did (Gen. 3:7) or shift the blame to someone else (Gen. 3:12-13). There's no indication she ever considered suicide, not did she retreat into alcoholism, although Eli, the high priest, mistakenly thought she had been drinking when she came to the sanctuary and poured out her heart in prayer. Hannah didn't do any of these. She remained silent and clung to God. "In you, O Lord, I put my trust; Let me never be ashamed; Deliver me in Your righteousness. Bow down Your ear to me; deliver me speedily; be my rock of refuge; a fortress of defense to save me" (Psalm 31:2-3).

Squelch shame. Ask the Holy Spirit to help you firmly grasp the following truths. Please don't be in a hurry to complete this lesson.

Truth # 1: God is eager to restore you

Shame is no respecter of persons. Often shame brings deep feelings of guilt and unworthiness. This, in turn, leads to self-hatred. Why did the apostle Peter struggle with shame? Read Matt. 26:69-75.

The apostle Paul could have allowed his ugly past to define him and strap shame on him. What did he regret? Read 1 Timothy 1:13.

Peter and Paul could have allowed shame to rob them of the joy of forgiveness. Allowing shame could have resulted in a continuous battle with self-condemnation. Instead, they laid their guilt and shame at the foot of the cross, found restoration, and praised God. (1 Timothy 1:14-17)

Maybe you feel shame due to personal regrets, failures, or unconfessed sin. Do you or others say you ruined your life and destroyed hope for anything good? God is eager to restore you.

Write your name in the blanks and prayerfully profess this truth out loud. "Here is a trustworthy saying that deserves full acceptance: Christ Jesus came into the world to save sinners of whom _____ is the worst. But for that very reason _____ was shown mercy so that in _____, the worst of sinners, Christ Jesus might display his unlimited patience as an example for those who would believe on him and receive eternal life. Now to the King eternal, immortal, invisible, the only God, be honor and glory for ever and ever. Amen" (1 Timothy 1:14-17).

Truth #2: God loves you

When Adam and Eve ate the forbidden fruit, their eyes were open. They learned they were naked and for the first time, they experienced shame and guilt.

In a desire to cover their nakedness, they "sewed fig leaves together and made themselves loincloths" (Genesis 3:7). Their own remedy for guilt was "aprons." (KJV) Realizing that the leaves couldn't cover their shame, they "hid themselves from the presence of the LORD" (vs. 8). But God, in His mercy and grace, came to them. He did not leave them to hiding in fear and shame. He reached out to them.

He covered not just their private parts but their bodies, making clothes for them. Many commentators believe their clothes were made from animals sacrificed for that purpose. It is a foreshadowing of the gospel in which Christ, the blameless Lamb of God, was sacrificed to cover and atone for our sins.

"This is love: not that we loved God, but that _____ and sent his Son as an atoning sacrifice for our sins" (1 John 4:10).

The word "atonement" means to cover. Jesus' blood covered and removed the guilt and shame of your sins. Just like Adam and Eve, your efforts cannot cover sin, guilt, or shame. Your righteousness, or right standing with God, required slaying an innocent substitute. (2 Corinthians 5:21)

"God so _____ the world that he gave his one and only _____ that whoever believes in him will not perish" (John 3:16). This agape love was coined by the Greeks because there was no other word to express God's unfathomable love God for sinners.

Agape love seeks the highest good for the other person…always…no matter what. Agape love does not consider the worth of its object but is a love by choice. God chose to love you in spite of your sins. (Romans 5:8) How might this truth demolish shame in your life?

Consider this. The universe has approximately 100 billion galaxies. Each galaxy has a diameter millions of miles wide! Imagine Love's Presence everywhere. Is there any place you can go to hide your shame from God? Why not? Read Psalm 139:7-10.

There are 7.2 billion people on the planet earth. Still, God values each individual. To what extent?

Luke 12:7

Zephaniah 3:17

The word rejoice literally means "to twirl." Take a moment to imagine the Lord's great gladness! He sings over you and twirls about you.

In *The Singing God*, Sam Storms explains, "It's as if God says, 'I love you so much that I can't find words to express it. You so perfectly satisfy My every desire and fulfill My every wish that I simply long to embrace you in My arms and quietly enjoy your presence'". God's unconquerable, omnipresent love sends shame running.

How does Romans 8:38-39 explain God's unconquerable love for you? Personalize this marvelous truth. Declare it out loud. Memorize it!

Walk in Freedom

Describe the person released from shame according to Romans 4:7-8.

Confront your shame with Jesus, your strong advocate. What does He promise?
Isaiah 50:7-9a

Isaiah 61:7

The "blessed" person experiences deep peace and joy. If you are not, ask the Holy Spirit to make these truths real to you. Ask Him what may be hindering you from receiving them. Reviewing the truths in Lesson 2 may also be helpful.

Live free from a yoke of shame. Though you may regret it, you can't undo your past. But in the light of God's mercy, you can give yourself the gift of self-forgiveness. God is nearby, waiting to hear you call. He will cleanse your conscience. (Hebrews 9:14; Psalm 32:3-5; 34:5)

Please set aside time to get quiet, without distractions. Begin with this prayer:

I praise You, Jesus, for being my advocate. Thank You for standing with me to confront my shame. I put my trust in You, the sovereign Lord, to help me, redeem me, and set me free. Thank You, Jesus, for Your sacrifice that redeems me. You are my

Advocate to stand between me and my accuser. In Your mighty name I pray, Amen.

Check any of the following lies that you believe.
__I'm unworthy of God's help.
__ I'm a disappointment to God, others, and myself.
__ I've ruined my life forever.
__ I'm undeserving of a better life.
__ If I were more spiritual, I wouldn't have all this heartache.
__ By punishing myself, I'm paying for my mistakes.
__ My prayers are not good enough for God to answer.
__ I'm not worthy of God's blessings.
__ I'm some kind of a martyr.

1. Prayerfully ask the Holy Spirit to help you remember the incident attached to each lie.
2. Forgive yourself. Bring your shame to the foot of the cross. (You may consider asking a spiritually mature friend or counselor to pray with you.)
3. Renounce the lies you have entertained about yourself and others related to the hurt.

Restoration may mean accepting the consequences of your wrong doing. The Lord may direct you to pay back some money, apologize, regain another person's trust, or correct a problem that you helped create. It may mean admitting you are wrong. It's a humbling experience, but it's like applying salve to your aching heart.

Truths to take away
1. God welcomes the humble. Only He can deliver me and cleanse me from shame. Jesus is my advocate.

2. Shame is defeated when it's brought to the foot of the cross and I acknowledge the power of the precious blood of Jesus.

3. The journey to freedom from shame is not easy, but it is God's best for me.

Embrace Your New Identity

Today's verse

"...let God remold your minds from within, so that you may prove in practice that the plan of God for you is good... and move toward the goal of true maturity" (Romans 12:2 Phillips).

Read: 1 Samuel 1

During Hannah's heartache, she maintained a clear perspective of how the Lord viewed her. She would not allow criticisms, negative labels, or barrenness to define her. Hannah believed she was made in the image of God and therefore, she was worthy of respect. (Genesis 1:26)

Hannah's spiritual identity grew rock solid. Evidence of this occurs when Eli accused Hannah of drunkenness. He was accustomed to people attending the festivals and drinking too much. Hannah boldly refuted him, "Not so, my lord. I am a woman who is deeply troubled. I have not been drinking wine or beer; I was pouring out my soul to the Lord. Do not take your servant for a wicked woman; I have been praying here out of my great anguish and grief" (1 Samuel 1:15-16).

Heartache cannot change the fact that you are "a new creation in Christ" (2 Corinthians 5:17). Even when Satan whispers: "loser," "unworthy," "despicable," "unaccepted," or "shameful," *in Christ* our noble worth never changes.

Listen to God's Word. He has the final say about your new identity. Let God remold your mind from within to find freedom and peace.

What God says about you

Gideon was the youngest in his family and came from the weakest clan. He did not have impressive credentials for leadership. Nevertheless, the Angel of the LORD viewed Gideon differently. He appeared to Gideon, and said "The LORD is with you, you mighty man of valor!" (Judges 6:12)

Gideon does not view himself as powerful or brave. Gideon had an identity crisis. He reminds the Angel of the Lord that he's personally incapable, and he's practically a nobody. (vs. 15) Also, Gideon's confidence in the Lord was low. He felt that the Lord had forsaken the Israelites. (vs. 12)

The Angel of the Lord, now speaking to Gideon as the Lord Himself, commissioned Gideon to deliver the people of Israel. "Surely I will be with you, and you shall defeat the Midianites as one man." (vs.16)

When you understand your identity "in Christ" you do not rely upon human wisdom and abilities. Remember you have been blood-bought by Jesus. You have divine potential and honor. As the Lord's adopted child, He has given you new names. (Isaiah 62:2)

"royal priesthood, people belonging to God" 1 Peter 2:9 -

"God's children, heirs of God, co-heirs of Christ" Romans
8:16, 17-

"chosen, holy, dearly loved" Colossians 3:12-

"God's workmanship" Ephesians 2:10-

"more than conquerors" Romans 8:37-

Which of these names is most meaningful to you?
Why?

From ashes to beauty-celebrate who you are in Christ

The Lord replaces your ashes for a crown of beauty.
(Isaiah 61:3) Each truth below describes the beauty of your
spiritual identity in Christ. If your emotions are not
brought under the authority of God's Word, confusion will
cloud the truth.

Write a response to the Lord for each identity truth that
describes you.

I am adopted by God. Ephesians 1:5

I am forgiven by God for all my sins. 1 John 2:12;
Colossians 2:13,14

I am seen by God as holy, blameless, above reproach.
Colossians 1:21, 22

I am sealed with God's Holy Spirit. Ephesians 1:13

I am called to accomplish God's purpose. Romans 8:28

I am justified-declared right in God's sight. Romans 5:1

I am sanctified-set apart by God's Spirit. 1 Corinthians 6:11

I am redeemed-bought with Christ's blood. Ephesians 1:7

I am cleansed by Christ's blood for all my sin.1 John 1:7

I am complete in Christ. Colossians 2:10

I am confident that God will complete the good work He started in me. Philippians 1:6

What difference would believing these truths make in your heartache?

Share with a friend this week one "new name" the Lord has given you and why it gives you confidence and hope. Owning God's perspective of yourself will change you. Be patient and diligent with this transformational process. Remember, your work is to believe God's Word; He will do the changing within you!

Dear Father, I praise You for my new identity. Thank You for my beautiful, new names! I open my arms and my heart to receive all You have for me. I believe You fully delight in me. Write upon my heart who You say I am. Each day help me celebrate my new names. In Jesus' precious name, Amen.

Truths to take away

1. By accepting Jesus as my Savior and committing myself to Him through faith, I am a new creation in Christ.

I possess new names and a new identity! (1 Corinthians 5:12)

2. God evaluates me differently than others or myself.

3. My new identity becomes steadfast as I renew my mind with God's truths.

4. As I celebrate who I am in Christ, confidence rises up and hope leads me forward.

Great Trials Precede Great Faith

Today's verse
"Take up the shield of faith, with which you can extinguish all the flaming arrows of the evil one" (Ephesians 6:16).

Read: 1 Samuel 1

Devout Israelite parents were expected to commit their firstborn son to the Lord. (Exodus 22:29) Hannah's prayer went further. Though she did not use the word "Nazarite," Hannah clearly dedicated her son's entire life for service to the Lord. Her vow demonstrates sterling trust in God. (1 Samuel 1:11) She modeled how to "lean on, trust in, and be confident in the Lord with all your heart and mind, not relying on your own insights or understanding" (Proverbs 3:5).

Today, discover how God's Word awakens our faith and strengthens it for dark times. Believing God's truths helps us gain understanding and insights about His good and greater purposes. Only then, will we be able to walk in freedom and peace while we're hurting.

Your faith must be tested

Hannah lived in a nation much like ours. It was consumed with materialism and devastated by spiritual brokenness. Hannah needed faith in the Lord more than ever. She prayed with humble tears, and God graciously sheltered her in His powerful Presence.

"Faith must be tested because it can only become your intimate possession through conflict." (Oswald Chambers)

What does 1 Peter 1:6-7 say about faith?

What does 2 Timothy 4:7 compare living by faith to? A "_____" and a "_____."

Write faith's definition from Hebrews 11:1 (NLT). Refer to www.biblegateway.com for other Bible translations.

"Confidence" in Greek was used in the technical sense of a "title deed." A deed is a legal paper that proves you possess what you have received; it's assurance. In other words, faith is assurance of "things hoped for."

Why do you think the devil tries diligently to shipwreck your faith?

Consider Ephesians 6:14-17 which states several spiritual weapons you possess to fight against demonic spirits. Where does faith enter in?

Heartache will strengthen your faith if you listen to and obey God's Word.

During our marriage struggles, the Lord faithfully awakened fresh faith for my marriage. As I met with Him one early morning, He highlighted an unusual Scripture. "The voice of the Lord strikes with flashes of lightening. The voice of the Lord shakes the desert... The voice of the Lord twists the oaks and strips the forests bare. And in his temple all cry, 'Glory!'" (Psalm 29: 7-9)

My heart leapt. This metaphor of God's power and sovereignty stirred hope within. I believed the God of break through was saying He would bring life into the dry, arid places of my marriage. Confidence and hope rose up within me.

This specific Word became my lifeline. It sustained faith-filled expectations that my marriage would be healed. When my feelings resisted, I talked to God about them and He always led me back to His truth.

Remaining in God's Word reshaped my understanding about my role in marriage. I was called to serve my husband "as unto the Lord." God always provided grace to do that.

Where does faith come from? (Romans 10:17)

How does Deuteronomy 32:47 describe God's Word?

Why is simply hearing God's Word not enough? (Hebrews 4:3)

According to Matthew 7:24-27 why will listening to, depending upon, and obeying God's Word strengthen your faith and overcome Satan's obstacles?

Memorizing God's Word also grows faith. "The Law of the Lord is perfect, restoring the whole person, making wise the simple, rejoicing the heart, enlightening the eyes" (Psalm 19:7-8 AMP). Will you commit to memorizing one Scripture this week?

Suffering and sorrow can strengthen your faith

Godly Jewish parents took time to teach their children prayers, study the Torah with them and speak blessings for their future. As early as three-years-old, Hannah would have heard stories about God's power, deliverances and triumphs. She learned of Joshua's leadership and how he held to God's Word (Joshua 8:34-35); She learned how Joseph rose from prison to prominence, refusing to allow bitterness to color his life. (Genesis 39-41); Hannah heard about Abram's great faith (Genesis 12:1-4) and his example of intercession (Genesis 18:16-33). Hannah believed "as for God, his way is perfect; the word of the LORD is flawless. He is a shield for all who take refuge in him" (2 Samuel 22:31).

During heartache, God and His Word can grow more valuable than anyone or any earthly thing. You can exclaim with the Psalmist, "Oh, how I love your law!" (119:97) What benefits is God's Word offering you? Read Psalm 119:98-100.

1.
2.
3.

During my friend's healing journey, Shari experienced sadness, loneliness, rejection, fear, and anxiety. Many times she cried out to the Lord for help, "I can't do this without you. I know you are the only One who can set me free."

She writes, "One morning when my heart was sad and hurting, I went straight to the Lord. He showed me a part of my sadness was about my mom not talking to me and my family for three years. I called Jane, my friend and counselor, and she prayed with me. I cried deeply, crying out to Jesus to help me and heal me. The Lord gave me His promise from Hebrews 13:5: 'never will I leave you; never will I forsake you.' This meant under no circumstances would God be leaving me alone, neither would God abandon me. God's truth filled my heart with peace."

Psalm 119 tells you benefits of reading and believing God's Word.

Verse 28: When your soul is weary with sorrow, God's Word will

Verse 43: When you feel hopeless, God's Word

Verse 105: When you need direction in dark places, God's Word provides

Verse 143: In trouble, God's Word becomes your

Verse 165: When you're facing fearful situations, God's Word offers

Verse 171: God's Word encourages a spirit of

My 14-year-old daughter's foolish choices caused me anxious thoughts. For months, I'd frequently wake up during the night and pray. This journal entry was written during those dark hours.

"Curled up on the couch, I began rehearsing my fears. When I finished, a long lonely silence met me. Then finally I heard a whisper, 'Be anxious for nothing. The Lord is near' (Philippians 4:6).

"I repeated that truth over and over. God's gentle, yet authoritative words infused me with assurance. I believed God's nearness to my daughter kept her safe. Trusting His Word, my burden lifted."

"If your Word hadn't delighted me so, I would have given up when the hard times came" (Psalm 119:92 MSG).

Did my faith ever weaken while waiting for my daughter's life to change? Yes! But, rather than cling to doubt, I chose to believe what God told me to be true. I thanked Him and praised Him. I was assured His answer would come in His time and His way.

What does God promise when you earnestly seek Him by faith? (Hebrews 11:6)

"We can be assured there is no reluctance on God's part to give us whatever is good for us. He does not need to be coaxed, for He is not capricious. Prayer is not a means of extorting blessing from unwilling fingers…The necessity must lie in us, not in God. It is not God who is under the test, but our own spiritual maturity." (J. Oswald Sanders)

Strengthen your faith with God's promises

"There is great value in searching the Scriptures. There may be a promise in the Word that exactly fits your situation, but if you are unaware of it, you will be like a prisoner in a dungeon." (Charles Spurgeon)

Believing God's Word guards you from becoming a prisoner to negative emotions. "As for God, his way is perfect: The Lord's word is flawless; he shields all who take refuge in him " (Psalm 18:30 KJV).

Fill in the words for each Scripture promise.

a. "God has said, '_____ will I _____ you; _____ will I forsake you'" (Hebrews 13:5-6).

b. "The Lord is my _____, my _____, and my _____..." (Psalm 18:2).

c. "If God is ____ _____, who can be against me? (Romans 8:31).

d. God "is able to do immeasurably _____ than all we _____ or imagine" (Ephesians 4:32).

e. "There is no _____ for those in Christ Jesus" (Romans 8:1).

f. "God loves me with an _____ love and continues to show _____" (Jeremiah 31:3).

g. "The plans of the Lord _____ firm _____" (Psalm 33: 11).

Which promise(s) are you taking hold of and believing with all your heart?

To "see" these promises in your heartache may be difficult, but you may be certain they are true. "For no matter how many promises God has made, they are "Yes" in Christ. And so through him the "Amen" is spoken by us to the glory of God" (2 Corinthians 1:20).

"Faith is not a sense, nor sight, nor reason, but taking God at His Word." (Christmas Evans)

Dear Lord, Thank You for Your precious and powerful Word. Please help me mediate on Your truth and believe it wholeheartedly. Cause Your words to come alive in my heart. Strengthen my faith. I want to be able to echo the words of Paul, "I have fought the good fight...I have kept the faith" (2 Timothy 4:7). Amen.

Truths to take away

1. Troubles provide a pathway for my faith to be tested, strengthened, and proved genuine.

2. God's Word mixed with faith provides a spiritual anchor, keeping my emotions in balance and providing freedom and peace.

3. Standing firm in my faith is a battle.

Journal

Trouble Invites What-ifs and Other Questions

Today's verse

"For my thoughts are not your thoughts, neither are your ways my ways, declares the Lord. As the heavens are higher than the earth, so are my ways higher than your ways and my thoughts than your thoughts" (Isaiah 55:8-9).

Read: 1 Samuel 1

The day finally arrived. The Sovereign Lord rewarded Hannah's faith and she conceived Samuel. His name means "Heard by God" (1 Samuel 1:20). However, this precious gift probably filled Hannah with concerns and worrisome "what-ifs." Why?

Young Samuel would be sent to the temple to be trained and raised by an elderly priest who was guilty of not being able to train his own sons (1 Samuel 3:13). They were evil men who had no regard for the Lord. (1 Samuel 2:12) While nursing Samuel those three precious years, Hannah must have had wondered, *What-if my*

impressionable, precious son is harmed by Eli's ungodliness?
Should I have made that vow? Did I hear the Lord correctly?

Can you imagine placing your precious three-year-old into the hands of immoral, selfish people? If you were in Hannah's shoes, what might you be thinking?

Entertaining what-ifs weakens our faith and steals our peace. Unanswered questions can build a wall between you and God. Have your wonderful expectations turned into perplexing questions? Today, let's consider why God allows them.

Jesus welcomes what-ifs

During a Bible study, my friend Ardell opened her hands in prayer as a sign of surrender. The group leader prayed, but Ardell couldn't hear a word due to loud, accusing voices filling her mind. She stared at her open hands and thought, *so much loss.* Ardell wanted to close them tight because she feared what God might choose to fill them with.

What-if He fills them with more loss?
What-if He says Jesus is enough?
What-if my hopes and dreams are never realized?

As these questions swirled in Ardell's head she watched her fingers tighten, slowly shutting God out. Then she heard God's whisper..."Will you trust me?"

Ardell said, "In seconds, all His faithfulness and grace during my losses flashed through my mind. 'Yes. I trust you!' Although it was a weak 'yes,' my fingers relaxed and my hands stayed open."

Ardell clung to this truth: God's will is love, and His love is wise! It freed her from worrisome what-ifs.

What might the Lord be asking you to trust Him for? Are you in that place of fearing to fully surrender your will?

Consider John the Baptist. Sitting in a bleak dungeon, troubled and perplexed, John asks his friends to send a challenging question to Jesus. What does he ask? Read Matthew 11:3.

Certainly John wonders, *Why am I in here? Is Jesus really the Messiah? Why doesn't He get me out of this place?*
What challenging question(s) have you asked God recently?

How did John's question reflect confidence or lack of confidence in Jesus?

What is Jesus' answer? See Matthew 11:4-6.

Jesus did not scold John for questioning His identity, but Jesus tacks on a powerful message: "Blessed is he who is not offended because of Me" (Matthew 11:6 NKJV). "Blessed is the man who does not fall away on account of me." (NIV)

Do you think Jesus' answer comforted John or confused him? Why? (Remember, John is in prison, unsure of his fate.)

Jesus was saying, "John, will you still love me even though you may never see the fulfillment of your prayers, hopes and dreams? Will you still trust Me in spite of your fears?"
D. Martin Lloyd-Jones says, "It is a fundamental principle in the life and walk of faith that we must always

be prepared for the unexpected when we are dealing with God."

During Hannah's heartache, the Lord must have asked her the same, unorthodox question. "Will you love Me, Hannah, if I give you a son but you must give him back to Me? Will you let Me become more to you than having a son?" Hannah responded with a resounding "yes." "Give your maidservant a male child, then I will give him to the LORD all the days of his life" (1 Samuel 1:11.)

Hannah's prayer joined with God's will. Hannah's surrender was forged by years of prayer and intimacy with her God.

Are you entertaining what-ifs? What-if _____ happens to me? My loved one? My job? My career? My finances? Or what-if it doesn't happen?

The Lord allows questions and "what-ifs." He is never offended by them. Just like when your children come to you, any time of the day or night, you want to hear what worries them, how they are struggling.

The Lord never forgets

Unanswered questions and what-ifs in the midst of perplexing circumstances might cause you to think God has forgotten you. With the passing of time, human promises are usually not kept; not with God! He will do what He said He would do. "With the Lord a ____ is like a thousand years, and a thousand years are like a _____" (2 Peter 3:8 NIV).

Are you worried God has forgotten you? Are you fretful you will not receive what you need?

What do Matthew 6:33 and Hebrews 13:5 promise?

Consider this truth: "Behold, I have indelibly imprinted (tattooed a picture of) you on the palm of each of My hands." (Amp) Reflect on Spurgeon's insight: "I have graven thy person, thy image, thy case, thy circumstances, thy sins, thy temptations, thy weaknesses, thy wants, thy works; I have graven thee, everything about thee, all that concerns thee; I have put thee altogether there. Wilt thou ever say again that thy God hath forsaken thee when he has graven thee on his own palms?" (Isaiah 49:16)

How does this truth strengthen your confidence in God?

Consider this wisdom: "Some prayers are followed by silence because they are bigger than we can understand." (Oswald Chambers)

How would you explain that God's silence to Hannah's prayers was best? (Keep in mind that Samuel grew to become God's leader for Israel, a priest and a prophet who would change the course of a nation. And it all began with suffering.)

The great "I am"

God declared Himself "I Am" to Abraham when He promised that Abraham and his descendants would be delivered out of Egypt. "I Am" is associated with God's character as One who keeps His gracious provision of redemption. (Isaiah 53:1, 5, 6, 10) "I Am" translated "Yahweh" is the most significant name for God in the Old Testament. It occurs 6,823 times.

Yahweh takes into consideration the hows and whys behind every situation. "For My _____ are not your _____, neither are your _____ my ways, declares the Lord" (Isaiah 55:8 NIV).

What will you do with your unanswered questions and what-ifs? Yahweh desires for you to release all your worries, cares, fears....all your "what-ifs." He is calling, "Don't go to the what-if's, come to Me!"

You do it by obeying 1 Peter 5:7. Cast all your anxiety on Him because He cares for you. Casting your what-ifs upon God requires the same authority Jesus used in confronting demons.

Write out your concerns, your what-ifs and unanswered questions. Then begin casting with authority. Don't allow what-ifs and fear to steal your freedom and peace.

Great I Am, I praise You! When Your answers to my questions are silent or not what I want, please help me to trust You regardless. Help me believe that silence may be Your answer for Your greater kingdom purposes. Today, strengthen my faith to cast my what-ifs and questions upon You. I trust Your peace that surpasses understanding awaits me. In Jesus' name, Amen.

Truths to take away

1. God's will is love and His love is wise! Therefore, I can trust His silence.

2. God's purpose for what-ifs and unanswered questions is far greater than my personal fulfillment.

3. I've been given authority and power to cast all my concerns onto the Lord.

Journal

God's Good and Greater Purposes for Waiting

Today's verse
"Therefore the LORD is waiting to show you mercy, and is rising up to show you compassion, for the LORD is a just God. All who wait patiently for Him are happy" (Isaiah 30:18 HCSB).

Read: 1 Samuel 1

God's Word points us to an ironic truth. Instead of taking us out of trouble, often God is more interested in taking us *through* trouble. It may last a short time, or perhaps years, as in Hannah's case. Nevertheless, God brings about His greater good while we wait.

While waiting Hannah relied on the Lord's strength and grace. Rather than owning a victim mentality, she found hope and healing in the LORD of Hosts. "...are You not the God who is in heaven, and do You not rule over all the kingdoms of the nations? Power and might are in Your hand, and no one can stand against You" (2 Chronicles 20:6 HCSB). Hannah trusted the Lord's plans for her welfare

(Jeremiah 29:1). She triumphed in faith, praying without ceasing. She grew to know the Lord beyond head knowledge and beyond her pain. "He heals the brokenhearted and binds up their wounds" (Psalm 147:3 HCSB). The Lord gave Hannah fresh revelations of Himself and she sang His praises. (1 Samuel 2)

God promises that waiting is not in vain. "Since ancient times no one has heard, no ear has perceived, no eye has seen any God besides you, who acts on behalf of those who wait for Him" (Isaiah 64:4).

Beauty and benefits of waiting

Patience and Joy

The Apostle Peter describes the waiting process as "a spiritual refining process, with glory just around the corner" (1 Peter 4:12-13 MSG). The word glory in Greek is *doxa*. *Doxa* means possessing all the excellence of God: His patience and joy, love and goodness, compassion and mercy, and peace that surpasses understanding!

James 1:2-4 also describes what glory looks like when going through trials. What does it look like?

The KVJ version translates vs. 4, "But let patience have her perfect work, that ye may be perfect and entire, wanting nothing." Patience is not passively resigning to difficult circumstances. It is a positive steadfastness that bravely endures. If you are expressing patience, how does it give glory to God? (vs. 4)

Ally's infertility caused her to wait on God to become pregnant. Waiting used to mean sadness, confusion and anger. Not anymore. Ally shares her story.

103

I sat alone in my car with tears drenching my face. I cried out loud in desperation and anger, "Why God? Why me? Why us? This can't be true...oh God, how could you let my baby die?" When I couldn't cry anymore and my mouth lay silent, I heard these lyrics whisper through my car speakers, "When you don't know what to say, just say, Jesus, there is power in the name, the name of Jesus!" I began sobbing again, "Jesus, Jesus, Jesus..." over and over.

A few months earlier, my husband and I had our first OB appointment. We had seen our tiny baby's heart flickering on the sonogram machine. We felt pure joy and excitement. Now, we exited feeling hopeless, confused, and utter sorrow. The image of our lifeless baby shocked us beyond belief.

Life without our baby "Ellery" turned into a battle I suited up for every single day. I would think about how different my life would be with Ellery. Then sadness overwhelmed me and all I could whisper was the name "Jesus" over and over and over.

During my daily battles, I had conversations with Jesus ranging from anger and confusion to hopelessness. Jesus always listened and showed me grace, love and mercy. I was not fighting this battle alone. My prayers turned into thanksgiving, gladness, and hopefulness.

Infertility is teaching me that my satisfaction and happiness will not be found in baby Ellery, or any other baby for that matter, but in my Heavenly Father. He is my Ellery, and He is enough. I'm finding my joy is in Jesus. Yes, I still yearn for and pray every day for a healthy baby, but my prayers have transformed from begging to patiently asking and waiting.

Today, I'm confident and content in knowing God knows my every need. I believe He will provide a healthy baby for my husband and me someday. In my waiting, God continues to turn this painful process into something beautiful.

Patience is a godly character quality that is produced within as we spend time in the presence of the Lord.

Waiting in God's presence takes you beyond immediate problems and painful circumstances. Martin Luther said, "Being silent in God molds us into the right shape." It molds patience within to endure.

Is it any wonder why Hannah remained patient in her difficult relationships and barrenness?

"Rest in the Lord, wait patiently for Him" (Psalm 37:7 KJV). Resting in the Lord does not mean inactivity. What does James 1:2 tell you to do in response to trials?

How do you usually respond when the Lord takes you through trials?

"To count it all joy" surely does not refer to an emotional reaction. Kay Warren is a servant who fully trusts in the Lord. But she could not feel joy after her son committed suicide. She wrote, "Paul says, 'Always be full of joy in the Lord. I say it again-rejoice!' It seemed to indicate that everyone is supposed to be experiencing joy...and I was not. I got tired of that sense of failure. That's when I did a study and realized I had completely misunderstood joy. I wasn't experiencing it because I was going after the wrong thing. I was going after an emotion. And what God wanted to give me was Himself."

Like Kay, have you misunderstood your source of joy? Joy is not the absence of heartache. According to Psalm 16:11, where is joy found?

What can you rejoice in the Lord for today?

Intimacy with God and Strength

The Hebrew translation of "wait" has nothing to do with time. It means "to bind together" like the strands in a rope are intertwined.What evidence is there that Hannah had a consistent, intertwined relationship with the Lord? (1 Samuel 2: 1-2)

How would you describe your relationship with the Lord if you were bound together with Him, like strands of a rope?

A big benefit of being intertwined with the Lord is found in Isaiah 40:31(NKJV). "But those who wait on the Lord shall _____ their strength;They shall mount up with wings like eagles, They shall run and not be weary, They shall walk and not be faint."

Renew literally means to change clothes. Waiting on the Lord gives God the opportunity to exchange your weakness for His strength.

If eighty-five-year-old Catherine and I hadn't chatted at the store, I wouldn't have guessed she suffered with leukemia. Catherine carried a cheerful disposition that matched her outfit, and she enjoyed talking about her world-wide trips.

"You're so peaceful and full of life," I commented. "How do you manage so well?" She smiled and was thoughtfully silent.

"Every day before I get out of bed, I look up to the One who gives strength. I wait on Him. Then I put one foot in front of the other. He never leaves my side."

Practically speaking, what does waiting on the Lord require of you?

Lloyd John Ogilvie, says, "The period of waiting for the granting of some request is often rewarded by a far greater gift than what we asked for. The Lord Himself... Job could say, 'I have heard of You by the hearing of the ear, but now my eye sees You.'" (Job 42:5)

How might waiting transform your attitudes about life? About others? About God?

Beware: your way or God's way?

Waiting might invite self-protective thoughts that evolve into actions that draw us away from God's will. For example, When Saul sensed panic among his troops, he felt "compelled" to offer the burnt offering himself, a task only priests were allowed to perform. He feared losing control. Instead of gaining "the Lord's favor" (1 Samuel 13:12), he lost his leadership position. The LORD sought a man after His own heart and appointed David leader of His people.

If Hannah had acted impulsively instead of waiting on God for a child, what action might she have taken? (Recall what Sarah did in Genesis 16.)

"There is a way that seems right to a man, but in the end it leads to _____" (Proverbs 14:12).

When you have acted compulsively instead of waiting on God, what was the end result?

What self-protective or self-serving thoughts do you need to carefully pay attention to? See Proverbs 4:23.

Consider Mary and Martha's example of waiting. They thought Jesus had forgotten them. He was delayed for four days, Lazarus died, and so they blamed Jesus. John 11:15, 40 tells how Jesus responded to His disappointed, grieving followers. What powerful statements did He make?

When God has you wait, you might hear Jesus asking, "Do you really believe?" For Mary and Martha he said, "This sickness will not end in death" (vs. 4). If they had believed, what might they have said to Jesus when He arrived?

Has the Lord given you a promise related to your current heartache? "Make Your ways known to me, LORD; teach me Your paths. Guide me in Your truth and teach me…I wait for You all day long" (Psalm 25:4-5 HCSB). What is the Lord asking you to believe?

Dear Heavenly Father, help me wait with confident assurance knowing You are working out Your higher purposes for my life. I agree with David's prayer, "I trust in You, O LORD, You are my God. My times are in Your hands" (Psalm 31:14, 15). While waiting, help me to intertwine with You. I want to receive all I need from You, including Your perspective on waiting. Today, I choose to believe that You are working all things together for my good and for Your glory! In Jesus' name, Amen.

Truths to take away

1. Waiting always has greater purposes than what I can see. God uses waiting to transform my life and bring Him glory.

2. My waiting process is meant to lead me to the Lord and intertwine my heart with His.

3. "After a little while" of waiting, the Lord will "restore you and make you strong, firm and steadfast" (1 Peter 5:10).

Journal

Living Abandoned to God

Today's verse
"Whom have I in heaven but You? And I have no delight or desire on earth beside You. My flesh and my heart may fail, but God is the rock and firm strength of my heart, and my portion forever" (Psalm 73:25-26 AMP).

Read: 1 Samuel 1

Hannah's heartache propelled her to live in total abandonment to God. Overflowing love for God is expressed in her vow. "O LORD of Heaven's Armies, if you will look upon my sorrow and answer my prayer and give me a son, *then I will give him back to you. He will be yours for his entire lifetime...*" (verse 11, NLT). Taking a Nazarite vow on behalf of someone else is found no other place in the Bible!

Some interpret Hannah's vow as "making a deal with God" or "negotiating with God." At first glance it may appear that way, but to be willing to forego the pleasure of rearing her son and enjoy watching him grow up demonstrates ultimate sacrifice.

Hannah's "deep anguish" doesn't mean she was angry. Or, as she "wept bitterly" (vs. 10) doesn't mean she was resentful. Jesus, in His humanity, felt "deeply distressed" and "exceedingly sorrowful." Three times Jesus prays to His Father, "If you are willing, take this cup from me. Yet, not as I will, but as You will" (Matthew 26:37, 39 NKJV).

One saint stated, "Anguish is considered nothing less than a compassionate gift from God." The Lord's wisdom creates an inner anguish which fuels our prayers and generates an eagerness for God's will and His kingdom to come. Hannah and Jesus possessed the gift of anguish.

Hannah cried out "Lord of hosts" (vs. 11), *Yahweh Tsebaoth*, meaning "ultimate power over the whole universe and every living creature!" God is Hannah's portion! (Lamentation 3:24) She relies on Him for wisdom, power, and security. (Proverbs 18:10)

You may think, *Is it really possible to live like Hannah, totally abandoned to God?* Can my desire for harmonious relationships, good health, and financial security become *less* important than being consumed with God and His eternal purposes? Let's begin to learn how and why this kind of heart attitude is possible in order to experience freedom and peace.

A tender, delicate heart

This verse describes Hannah. "Delight yourself in the Lord and He will give you the desires of your heart" (Psalm 37:4). One meaning for the Hebrew word "delight" is "tender." Hannah's tender heart was gentle and flexible, the opposite of hard, callous, and resisting. Hannah's unusual vow reflected tenderness toward the Lord.

In Hebrew, delight also means "delicate." A delicate heart is sensitive and attentive to the Lord's ways. Such as the psalmist expressed, "I will praise the LORD, who

113

counsels me; even at night my heart instructs me" (Psalm 16:7).

Combine tender and delicate and you have a heart which quickly responds to the Lord. Your thoughts constantly turn to Him. He cheers your heart even when other things are oppressing you. You do all that you can for Him purely because He is your delight. Does that describe your heart? Why or why not?

A jogging enthusiast stated his delight in running, "I think about my morning jog when nature and my body awaken in harmony. I think about how far I will run and where I will run. I enjoy pleasant thoughts of getting away from life's daily responsibilities." Who or what do your thoughts frequently turn to?

There's nothing wrong with delighting yourself in your spouse, your children, your profession, social activities, etc. However, when you become obsessed and preoccupied with them, to the extent that they control your time, emotions, and thoughts, you have forgotten that God is better.

David delighted in the Lord during a plethora of troubles instead of fretting and envying. Fret literally means "to be furious," "boiling." Becoming obsessed with what others may be doing or saying, which may be causing your heartache, takes your focus off the Lord. So he quickly prescribed a divine antidote. "Delight yourself ___ _____ _____ and He will give you the desires of your heart" (vs:4). Change your focus to the Lord and, in doing so, your emotions and thoughts will become aligned with His. He becomes the author of your desires.

Job delighted in the Lord. He calls upon the Lord Almighty and compared Him to gold and silver. (Job 22:25-26) How do these verses apply to the person who delights in the Lord?

Whatever you delight yourself in will powerfully influence your heart. How do you relate to this truth?

If you choose to delight in the Lord, what "good" desires might you give less attention to?

Who do you seek to please first? Yourself or God? Others or God?

A humble heart

Humility and delighting in the Lord go hand in hand. Hannah reflected a spirit of humility when three times she addressed herself as a "Maidservant." (1 Samuel 1:11 NKVJ)

"Maidservant" implies "the least, insignificant, slave." A.C. Dixon, says, "The waters of God's blessings flow downward, and he who would drink them must stoop." Perhaps that's why God used Hannah as He did. Hannah quietly put aside self and submitted to God's desires.

According to Psalm 149:4, how does the Lord respond to humility?

The word "salvation" literally means "deliverance, victory, protection, strength!" "He [God] says, 'I live in a high and holy place, but I also live with people who are sad and humble. I give new life to those who are humble and to those whose hearts are broken'" (Isaiah 57:15 NCV).

Explain how having a humble spirit is essential to experiencing freedom and peace?

When threatened, challenged or called to account for your actions, a humble response is gentle and composed. Do your responses to heartache reflect humility?

How can humility transform your view of trouble or a troublesome person?

How does possessing humility make it possible for you to commit a troubling situation or a difficult relationship to God?

Better than an answer to prayer

Like Hannah, I felt deep anguish and cried bitterly during my teens' rebellion. I prayed and prayed for their attitude and their behavior to change. However, they seemed to remain the same. Growing more and more frustrated and discouraged, I requested prayer support from "Breakthrough," an international intercessory prayer team.

I believed more prayer would change them. Ironically, within a short time, my heart began to change!

In my quiet times I was impressed to dwell on the names of God. I discovered each name explains God's nature and how He cares for us. For example, *Jehovah Yireh*: the God who sees/provides. *Jehovah Rapha*: the God who heals. *Jehovah Tsidkenu*: the Lord our righteousness. *Jehovah Shamma*: the Lord who is present. *Jehovah Rohi*: the Lord is my shepherd.

As the Lord became bigger and more beautiful in my mind and heart, I found myself echoing David's prayers: "My soul thirsts for you;" "My body longs for you" (Psalm 63). I couldn't get enough of Him! He became my daily bread (John 6:48).

Delighting in the Lord, I felt He was tenderly wiping my tears. Focusing on God alone brought peace. Fearful "what-ifs" about my children's future lost their grip. The Lord turned my darkness to light. I was convinced God was working all things for His own perfect will. (Romans 8:28-29)

Charles Spurgeon said, "He that humbles himself under the hand of God shall not fail to be enriched, uplifted, sustained, and comforted by the ever-gracious One." When your heart is set on walking blamelessly before the Lord, your delight is only in what He desires. It changes how you pray and what you pray for.

What is your prayer focus today? Is it your pain, your fears, the unfairness of your situation?

Explain how "delighting in the Lord" will help redirect your prayers.

Why does delighting in the Lord assure you will receive His best? "He will fulfill the desire of those who fear Him" (Psalm 145:19).

Practical steps to help delight in the Lord

To delight in the Lord is another way of saying, "I cherish You Lord." It is a perfect "thank You." Mary Fletcher, a 17th century Methodist preacher, explained, "The soul who keeps the presence of God by a loving recollection, by faith and silence before him, enters into God as His strong habitation."

Cultivating delight in the Lord takes time and commitment. David, a man after God's heart, gave practical help.

Psalm 5:3: What did David do first thing in the morning?

Psalm 119:58: How did David approach God?

Psalm 59:16: When David was in the Lord's presence, what did he enjoy doing?

Psalm 55:17: What did David do when he felt heartache and distress?

Do you want your fondest desire to be the Lord, to delight in Him? Then pray this prayer.

O Lord, make my heart tender and delicate. I desire humility. May I sing like David: "You, LORD, are all I want! You are my choice, and you keep me safe. You make my life pleasant, and my future is bright" (Psalm 16:5-6, CEV). In Jesus' name, Amen.

Truths to take away

1. A heart that delights in the Lord is tender, gentle, and flexible to God's ways.

2. How I spend my time, and with whom, reflects and impacts the desires of my heart.

3. Delighting in God is often better than an answer to prayer!

Journal

Persevering in Prayer and Praise

Today's verse

"Keep on asking and it will be given you; keep on seeking and you will find; keep on knocking [reverently] and [the door] will be opened to you. For everyone who keeps on asking receives; and he who keeps on seeking finds; and to him who keeps on knocking, [the door] will be opened" (Matthew 7:7-8).

Read: 1 Samuel 1; 2:1-10

Hannah prayed without ceasing, remaining in perfect responsiveness to the Lord. "I lift my eyes unto the hills, Where does my help come from? My help comes from the Lord, the Maker of heaven and earth" (Psalm 121:1).

"Praying always with all prayer and supplication in the Spirit" (Ephesians 6:18 KJV), Hannah grew from strength to strength. Prayer became as natural as breathing.

In today's lesson you will learn what it means to "keep asking, keep seeking, and keep knocking." You will discover why praise and thanksgiving bring spiritual freedom and peace. This lesson may take more than one sitting. Allow the Spirit to set your pace.

Keep asking

In *The Washington Post*, an article told about a 15-year-old girl who sent and received 6,473 cell phone text messages in a month. Remarking about her constant communication with friends, she said, "I'd die without it." The average teen sends 3,339 texts per month.

Digital conversation illustrates what prayer could and should be. Paul says, "[We] do not cease to pray for you" (Colossians 1:9) and "Pray without ceasing" (1 Thessalonians 5:17). Missionary Frank Lauback used to "shoot" prayers all day long. He was "texting" God, in a sense, staying in constant communication with Him.

Don't allow heartache to discourage you and stop praying. James 4:2 states, "You don't have what you want because you don't ask God for it."

Take a moment to ask. What is it you want?

What does James 4:3 say hinders your prayers from being answered?

What else may hinder prayer?
Isaiah 59:1-2

1 Peter 3:7

Proverbs 28:9

"This is what I want you to do: Ask the Father for whatever is in keeping with the things I've revealed to you. Ask in my name, according to my will, and he'll most certainly give it to you. Your joy will be a river overflowing its banks!" (John 16:24 The Message)

What is the outcome of your asking if you ask according to God's will?

Perhaps you say, "I have healthy motives, and I believe I'm praying according to God's will, why don't I receive an answer or see any change?" Have you grown weary praying? "...the Spirit helps us in our _____.

We do not know what we ought to pray for, but the _____ himself intercedes for us with groans that words cannot express" (Romans 8:26). It is okay to run out of words while praying. You have the absolute assurance that the Spirit helps you in your weakness.

A seasoned prayer, Charles Spurgeon, offered this suggestion, "Though your words are broken, and your sentences disconnected, if your desires are earnest, God will not mind how they find expression. If you have no words, perhaps you will pray better without them than with them."

Judy's husband has Alzheimer's disease. His need for Judy's help and patience increases daily. When Judy feels overwhelmed, she simply prays staccato prayers throughout the day, "Jesus, help!"

According to Psalm 141:2, how does the Lord view prayer, even staccato prayers?

Keep seeking

A large part of seeking God's answer is actually seeking Him, as Hannah beautifully illustrated. Consequently, Hannah's heart was united with God's heart. She didn't want *any* answer, she wanted God's answer. After years of asking, Hannah named her son "Samuel" which means "heard of God."

Nearly all Old Testament Scriptures using the word "seek" refer to seeking God. Zephaniah 2:3: "Seek the LORD, all you humble...you who do what he commands."

Deuteronomy 4:29: "If you seek the LORD your God, you will find him if you look for him with all your heart and with all your soul."

Psalm 27:8:"My heart says of you, 'Seek his face!' Your face, LORD, I will seek."

Explain in your own words how seeking God will change your will from asking what self wants to what God wants.

Keep knocking

Jesus told a parable to illustrate the importance of praying with persistence.

"Jesus said to his disciples, 'Suppose one of you should go to a friend's house at midnight and say, "Friend, let me borrow three loaves of bread. A friend of mine who is on a trip has just come to my house, and I don't have any food for him!" And suppose your friend should answer from inside, "Don't bother me! The door is already locked, and my children and I are in bed. I can't get up and give you anything." Well, what then? I tell you that even if he will not get up and give you the bread because you are his friend, yet he will get up and give you everything you need because you are not ashamed to keep on asking'" (Luke 11:5-8 GNT).

Jesus said the man's request was answered due to his persistence. (vs. 8) What does He go on to say about persistence in vvs. 9-10?

Jesus encourages persistent prayer by reminding us of His nature. Who does He compare Himself to and how does this encourage you to keep knocking? Read vvs. 11-13.

Knocking suggests urgent and persistent prayers. In other words, once you see the breakthrough is within reach-keep asking, but with greater urgency. According to Mark 11:20-26, Jesus said, "Whatever, you ask for in prayer, believe that you have received it and it will be yours." Why is asking, seeking, and knocking with faith inseparable?

"Believing what God says in His Word is faith. If I am to have faith when I pray, I must find some promise in the Word of God on which to rest my faith. Faith also comes through the Spirit. The Spirit knows the will of God, and if I pray in the Spirit, and look to the Spirit to teach me God's will, He will lead me in prayer along the line of that will, and give me faith that the prayer is to be answered; but in no case does real faith come by simply determining that you are going to get the thing that you want to get." (R. A. Torrey)

Are your prayers based upon faith in God's Word and led by the Spirit or by self-determination?

Praise and thanksgiving

The uplifting hymn, *Now Thank We All Our God*, was written by Martin Rinkart in the midst of his country's darkest moments. His hometown, Eilenburg, Germany, a walled city, was looked upon as a place of refuge and safety for thousands of refugees fleeing the attacks of warring armies. Overcrowded and under-supplied with food, sanitary facilities, and medical care, the walled city became, instead, a city of death. Plagues and pestilence raged through the crowded streets and homes, claiming hundreds of victims.

During three decades of devastation, Rinkart was a model to his weak and wary parishioners. He encouraged them to see that their circumstances were temporary, while God's blessings were eternal, transcending earth's difficulties. It was this confidence that allowed Rinkart to continue in his ministry to the sick and dying of Eilenburg, even through the terrible plague of 1637. The other pastors had died or fled, but Rinkart stayed alone. He buried close to 4,500 men, women, and children, sometimes conducting up to forty-five funerals a day. He even buried his wife.

Like the apostle Paul, Martin learned that nothing in life or death could separate him from the love of God he found through Jesus Christ. Therefore, he encouraged his people to turn their eyes from their own despair to the power and love of God. In the midst of their constant pain and suffering, he composed over sixty hymns of faith and hope. (Quoted from *Hymns of Faith and Inspiration*.)

Anne Graham Lotz states, "Praise is the switch that turns on the light in the darkness of your life." It is the best weapon against Satan. "He who _____ thank offerings honors me, and he _____ the way so that I may show him the _____ of

God" (Psalm 50:23). Remember salvation literally means "help, victory, deliverance."

Consider Joshua. His undersized and poorly equipped army praised God, and an unseen angelic army enabled them to achieve what they could never achieve in their own power (Joshua 6).

Consider Paul and Silas. While praying and singing hymns to God in prison, a violent earthquake shook the prison doors wide open. Everybody's chains came loose and many salvations followed. (Acts 16:25-26)

Consider King Jehoshaphat. His army faced three powerful armies. "We do not know what to do," he prayed. The Lord responded, "Do not be afraid; do not be discouraged. Go out to face them tomorrow, and the LORD will be with you." Jehoshaphat then appointed men to sing to the LORD and to praise him for the splendor of his holiness. They went in front of the army, saying, "Give thanks to the LORD, for his love endures forever" (2 Chronicles 20:2; 21-22). Worship at the front lines brought God's help, victory and deliverance.

Praise and thanksgiving may not change your circumstances, but it will change your perspective. It will bring you back into the presence of God. If you are feeling alone and discouraged, what does the psalmist tell you to do in Psalm 5:11?

Do you tend to worry about the future? Do you fear bad news? What amazing benefits do you receive by praising the Lord and keeping His commands? See Psalm 112:1-8.

"Hannah overlooks her gift and praises the giver; whereas most forget the giver and fasten only on the gift," said Matthew Henry. What attributes of God's character did Hannah praise? (1 Samuel 2:1-10)

Hannah rejoiced because "the Lord has made me strong" (2 Samuel 2:1 NLT). What else did Hannah praise God for in vvs. 2-10?

Praise God using Psalm 146. The psalmist praised the Lord for all the help He provides (vv. 1-3), for His presence (vv. 4-7), and for the future peace that He will establish (vv. 8-11).

God is good no matter what heartache you are experiencing. Even when you don't understand, you can say with Habakkuk, "Yet I will rejoice in the LORD, I will be joyful in God my Savior" (3:18).

God's Word is filled with praises by people who were faced with crushing heartaches, injustices, treachery, slander and many other difficult situation. They knew that the sacrifice of praise was a key to victory on their spiritual journey. Hannah was one.

To conclude this lesson, thank the Lord and praise Him as your expression of love and faith. Surrender to the plans He has for you. "...let the hearts of those who seek Yahweh rejoice...Remember the wonderful works He has done, His wonders, and the judgments He has pronounced" (1 Chronicles 16:10-12 HCSB).

Truths to take away

1. Asking with right motives, even when my prayers are weak or wordless, pleases God.

2. Seeking God, with persistence and patience, unites my heart and will to God's heart and will.

3. Praise is essential for inner strength and encouragement when I am experiencing heartaches.

Closing

As you conclude this study, consider Joseph's final words to his brothers who had sold him into slavery: "As for you, you meant evil against me; but God meant it for good, in order to bring it about as it is this day, to save many people alive" (Genesis 50:20). Joseph's life embraced God and trusted Him completely. Through his extremely difficult circumstances, he found amazing freedom and peace in the Lord.

As you face heartache, will you put complete confidence in God's goodness and perfect plans? The things that could destroy you can become building blocks for your freedom and peace. Continue your journey of faith looking for the hand of God in all circumstances, praying and praising Him. "I've told you all this so that trusting me, you will be unshakeable and assured, deeply at peace. In this godless world you will continue to experience difficulties. But take heart! I've conquered the world" (John 16:33 MSG).

CPSIA information can be obtained
at www.ICGtesting.com
Printed in the USA
FFOW05n1612200615